T0340115

Prison Pens

New Perspectives on the Civil War

SERIES EDITOR
Judkin Browning, Appalachian State University

SERIES ADVISORY BOARD
Stephen Berry, University of Georgia
Jane Turner Censer, George Mason University
Paul Escott, Wake Forest University
Lorien Foote, Texas A&M University
Anne Marshall, Mississippi State University
Barton Myers, Washington & Lee University
Michael Thomas Smith, McNeese State University
Susannah Ural, University of Southern Mississippi
Kidada Williams, Wayne State University

Prison Pens

Gender, Memory, and Imprisonment
in the Writings of
Mollie Scollay and Wash Nelson,
1863–1866

Edited by Timothy J. Williams and Evan A. Kutzler

The University of Georgia Press
ATHENS

© 2018 by the University of Georgia Press
Athens, Georgia 30602
www.ugapress.org
All rights reserved
Set in 10/13 New Baskerville by
Graphic Composition, Inc., Bogart, Georgia.

Most University of Georgia Press titles are
available from popular e-book vendors.

Printed digitally

Library of Congress Cataloging-in-Publication Data

Names: Williams, Timothy J. (Timothy Joseph), editor. | Kutzler, Evan, editor.
| Container of (work): Nelson, G. Washington. Correspondence. Selections. |
Container of (work): Scollay, Mollie. Correspondence. Selections.
Title: Prison pens : gender, memory, and imprisonment in the writings of Mollie Scollay
and Wash Nelson, 1863–1866 / edited by Timothy J. Williams and Evan A. Kutzler.
Description: Athens : The University of Georgia Press, [2018] | Series: New perspectives
on the Civil War era | Includes bibliographical references and index.
Identifiers: LCCN 2017024997 | ISBN 9780820351933 (hardback : alk. paper) |
ISBN 9780820351926 (pbk. : alk. paper) | ISBN 9780820351940 (ebook)
Subjects: LCSH: Nelson, G. Washington—Correspondence. | Scollay, Mollie—Correspondence.
| Prisoners of war—United States—Correspondence. | Women—Virginia—Correspondence.
| United States—History—Civil War, 1861–1865—Personal narratives, Confederate.
| United States—History—Civil War, 1861–1865—Prisoners and prisons.
Classification: LCC E467 .P93 2018 | DDC 973.7/820922 [B]—dc23
LC record available at https://lccn.loc.gov/2017024997

For D.E.M. and A.M.N.

Contents

Family History of Rev. George Washington Nelson Jr.

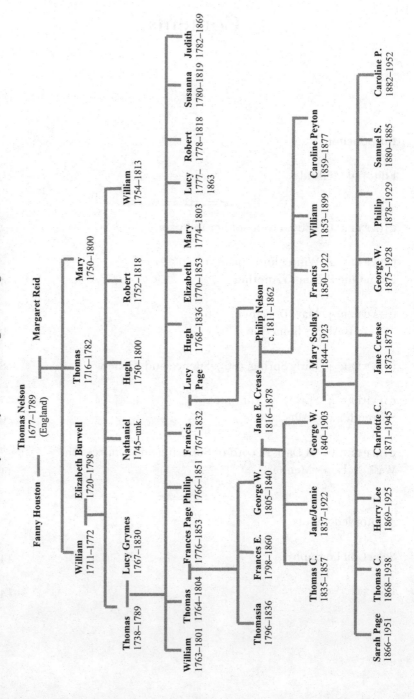

Prison Pens

Introduction

On April 12, 1865, Captain George Washington "Wash" Nelson Jr., a Confederate prisoner of war, had just heard that Middleway, West Virginia, where his cousin and fiancée, Mary Nelson "Mollie" Scollay, lived, had been the scene of a battle the previous August. Wash was perplexed. The two had been in touch during the months since the battle, but Mollie had said nothing of it. "Where were you, Mollie, when bullets were flying through your house and the porch blown up?" he asked in a letter. "You are quite a veteran." Of course he was right to worry. He read the news in prison; he heard stories about women on the home front, their hardships, their anxiety. Mollie (who, in fact, was fine) called this new normal "Confederate living." In a way, military occupation imprisoned her, as the Yankees imprisoned her fiancé. News of the Battle of Summit Point also moved Wash to reflect on their shared past, the many letters exchanged between the two lovers, and the constantly blighted hopes for reunion. "If we could be disinterested spectators of our own lives," he pondered, "the ups & downs and unexpected turns would be very amusing."[1] Fortunately, many letters that he and Mollie exchanged between 1863 and 1866 have survived, and while they are not exactly "amusing," they invite readers to be the disinterested spectators Wash and Mollie naturally could not be themselves.

The archival record of Wash and Mollie's love story begins in 1863—in the middle of the bloodiest war in American history. It was a year bounded in the winter by the Emancipation Proclamation and in the fall by the dedication of a sprawling national cemetery at Gettysburg to "a new birth of freedom" and the protection of a government "of the people, by the people, [and] for the people."[2] Union troops captured

---

1. Wash to Mollie, April 12, 1865, box 2, folder 38, Nelson Family Papers Ms1989-021, Special Collections, Virginia Tech, Blacksburg, Va. (hereinafter NFP).

2. Lincoln issued the preliminary Emancipation Proclamation on September 22, 1862, and the final proclamation on January 1, 1863. He delivered his famous address at Gettysburg on November 19, 1863. See James McPherson, *Battle Cry of Freedom: The Civil War Era* (Oxford, England: Oxford University Press, 1988), 557, 859.

Wash on October 26, 1863, in New Market, Virginia, a small village in the lower Shenandoah Valley, near Mollie's home. Over the next two weeks, Union officials moved Wash through Virginia and West Virginia into Ohio, where he spent the winter and early spring of 1864 surrounded by the wooden walls of Johnson's Island Military Prison and the watery barrier of Lake Erie. After being transferred to Point Lookout Prison in Maryland, he began showing symptoms of dysentery and was moved to the prison's hospital ward. Not long after recovering, he went to Fort Delaware, then to prisons in Union-controlled areas of South Carolina and Georgia. In the spring of 1865 he was sent back to Fort Delaware, where he remained until his release in June. In all, Wash was imprisoned for twenty months, spent time in six Union prisons, and traveled several thousand miles by road, rail, and water. During these tumultuous months, he and Mollie exchanged news about friends and family, discussed their reading lives, commented on the war, and expressed their love for one another. Their letters, as well as Wash's memoir, illuminate a war-torn world of intimacy, despair, loss, and reunion in the Civil War South.

Although what follows is their story, it was also the story of countless others, North and South, who lived through the Civil War. In particular, the experience of being a prisoner or knowing a prisoner was widespread. Perhaps as many as 420,000 Union and Confederate soldiers spent at least part of the war in captivity.[3] That number accounted for nearly one in seven soldiers, meaning that the suffering associated with prison experiences affected millions of people through the web of nineteenth-century social relations. In other words, it would have been difficult to find families, friends, neighbors, comrades, or lovers who did not, in one way or another, have a connection to Civil War prisons. The perspectives of Wash and Mollie therefore offer not only a new approach

---

3. Scholarly approximations of the number of men imprisoned during the war vary. William Best Hesseltine reported 420,000 prisoners in his seminal *Civil War Prisons: A Study in War Psychology* (Columbus: Ohio State University Press, 1998). More recently, Benjamin G. Cloyd has taken a more conservative approach, arguing that 410,000 soldiers were imprisoned during the Civil War, among whom approximately 56,000 died: 30,000 from the United States, and 26,000 from the Confederacy. See *Haunted by Atrocity: Civil War Prisons in American Memory* (Baton Rouge: Louisiana State University Press, 2010), 1. See also Charles W. Sanders Jr., *While in the Hands of the Enemy: Military Prisons of the Civil War* (Baton Rouge: Louisiana State University Press, 2005), 1. Although more Union soldiers died in Confederate camps than the other way around, the historical record is clear that prisons on both sides were grim.

to this ubiquitous wartime reality but also a needed addition to our understanding of the tensions that defined the Civil War era more broadly.

Families with Deep Southern Roots

Wash and Mollie descended from early Virginia's most prominent "first families," including the Randolph, Page, Harris, and, of course, Nelson families.[4] Born on May 27, 1840, in Hanover County, Virginia, Wash was the youngest child of Rev. George W. Nelson (1805–40) and Jane Crease Nelson (1816–78). Wash's father was an Episcopal priest and the grandson of General Thomas Nelson (1738–89), a signer of the Declaration of Independence.[5] He died just after Wash was born. Five years later, Wash's mother married Philip Nelson, her late husband's cousin and a planter owning twenty-six slaves in 1860.[6] They lived in the western district of Hanover County, located along the western edge of the state's Tidewater region and just north of Richmond, the capital and most populated city. Although Richmond was not the largest southern city in 1860, it offered valuable manufacturing, political, and cultural resources that made it appealing as the nascent capital of the fledgling Confederacy.[7]

---

4. Family genealogies have been invaluable. We have principally relied on T. K. Cartmell, *Shenandoah Valley Pioneers and Their Descendants: A History of Frederick County, Virginia from Its Formation in 1738 to 1908* (Winchester, Va.: Eddy Press Corp., 1909); William Ronald Cocke, *Hanover County Chancery Wills and Notes: A Compendium of Genealogical, Biographical and Historical Material as Contained in Cases of the Chancery Suits of Hanover County, Virginia* (Columbia, Va.: William Ronald Cocke III, 1940); William Samuel Harris, *The Harris Family: Thomas Harris, in Ipswich, Mass. in 1636. And Some of His Descendants, through Seven Generations, to 1883* (Nashua, N.H.: Barker & Bean, 1883); Katarina Wonders, "Prisoner of War: George Washington Nelson," unpublished essay, on the *Long Branch Plantation* website, http://www.visitlongbranch.org/wp-content/uploads/2015/07/P.O.W.-George -W.-Nelson1.pdf; Richard Channing Moore Page, *Genealogy of the Page Family in Virginia. Also a Condensed Account of the Nelson, Walker, Pendelton and Randolph Families* (New York: Press of the Publishers' Printing Co., 1893).

5. Harris, *Harris Family*, 80. Rev. George Washington Nelson was the priest in charge at Cople Parish in Westmoreland County, Va., between 1834 and 1840. Meade, *Old Churches and Families of Virginia* (Philadelphia: J. B. Lippincott & Co., 1861)2:147.

6. Philip Nelson was the son of Francis Nelson and Lucy Page. He was born at Mount Hair, Hanover County, Va., c. 1811. He and Jane Nelson had three children: Francis, Caroline, and William. Page, *Genealogy of the Page Family*, 177. 1850 and 1860 Federal Slave Schedule, Hanover County, Va.

7. Peter J. Parish, *The American Civil War* (New York: Holmes & Meier, 1975), 307. On Richmond's economic, political, and cultural importance, see Gregg Kimball, *American City, Southern Place: A Cultural History A History of Antebellum Richmond* (Athens: University

The region surrounding Richmond was also a major locus of plantation agriculture and slaveholding. According to the 1860 census, Hanover County had a population of 17,222 people, including 7,739 free
persons and 9,483 enslaved persons. The county's demographics resembled those along the black belt in Georgia, Mississippi, and Alabama
more closely than other counties of Virginia and Maryland. Slaveholders composed 51 percent of Hanover's free population; most of them
owned between one and ten slaves. Young Wash reaped the cultural and
political benefits sown by slaves in an economy that afforded white plant-
ers and their families economic and social status. He attended a private
academy—probably the Hanover Academy—and matriculated at the
University of Virginia in 1858, where he joined the Delta Kappa Epsilon
fraternity. Compared with other sons of slaveholding families, Wash's ambitions were modest: he wanted to enter the ministry and get married.[8]
After receiving a divinity degree from Virginia in 1860, he taught school
for one year in Caroline County, Virginia.[9] As a grown man, he was an
inch short of six feet tall with blue eyes, brown hair, and a florid complexion.[10]

Mollie was born on October 15, 1844 in Middleway, Virginia. She was
the youngest of three children of Samuel Scollay (1781–1857), a doc-
tor, and his second wife, Sally Page Nelson (1801–89).[11] A wealthy and
prominent member of the community, Scollay owned land throughout
Jefferson County. Located at the confluence of the Potomac and Shenandoah rivers, the county was bordered by Maryland to the northeast. The
geography of Jefferson County made it socially and culturally different

of Georgia Press, 2000), 5, 15–36; Jonathan Daniel Wells, *The Origins of the Southern Middle
Class, 1800–1861* (Chapel Hill: University of North Carolina Press, 2004), 7–8.

8. Peter S. Carmichael, *The Last Generation: Young Virginians in Peace, War, And Reunion*
(Chapel Hill: University of North Carolina Press, 2005), 74.

9. "George Washington Nelson," on *Long Branch Plantation* website, http://www
.visitlongbranch.org/history/people/gnelson/. There were two academies in Caroline
County in 1860: Caroline Academy and Rappahannock Academy. A. J. Morrison, *The Beginnings of Public Education in Virginia, 1776–1860: Study of Secondary Schools in Relation to
the State Literary Fund* (Richmond: Davis Pottom, Superintendent of Public Printing, 1917).

10. Compiled Confederate Service Records, National Archives and Records Administration.

11. Scollay was first married to Harriot Lowndes (1794–1835), of Georgetown, D.C.
They had five children: Charles Lowndes (1823–57); Anne Lloyd (1825–68); Samuel
Storrow (1827–31); Eleanor Grover (1829–55); and Elizabeth (1831–?). Only two chil-
dren from his second marriage lived to adulthood. The firstborn, Francis Nelson Scollay,
died in early childhood. When Scollay died in 1857, he had $100,000 to his name. Harris,
Harris Family, 76.

A view of Middleway, Virginia, during the Civil War.
James E. Taylor, *With Sheridan up the Shenandoah Valley in 1864.*
The Western Reserve Historical Society, Cleveland, Ohio.

from Hanover County, particularly in terms of slavery. In 1860, Jefferson County's total population was 14,535, including 10,575 free persons (which likely included free black persons), and 3,960 enslaved persons.[12] Over the course of Mary's childhood and youth, Middleway grew significantly, with residents numbering around 350 in 1840 and 446 in 1850, but slaveholding was less common there than in Hanover County.[13] In 1860, Mollie lived in Middleway, with her mother, older sister Harriot, and aunt, Frances B. Nelson. Sometimes Mollie referred to her home as Middleway, while other times she called it "Old Clip" or "Wizard's Clip," which derived from local folklore.[14]

Wash and Mollie belonged to the last generation of Virginians who came of age before the Civil War. The higher education that Wash received at the University of Virginia—a classical liberal arts education in ancient languages and literature, rhetoric, logic, oratory, science, and religion—emphasized republican leadership and celebrated individual ambition as a quintessentially manly trait. Christian religion grounded and tempered that ambition, compelling young men to seek "moral perfection" as Christian gentlemen.[15] Young women's education was equally

12. 1860 U.S. Census, Jefferson County, Va., population schedule. Prepared by Social Explorer, http://www.socialexplorer.com/tables/Census1860/R11389763?ReportId= R11389763 (accessed April 12, 2017).

13. Millard Kessler Bushong, *A History of Jefferson County, West Virginia* (Bowie, Md.: Heritage Books, Inc., 2002), 97.

14. Cartmell, *Shenandoah Valley Pioneers*, 241–42.

15. Carmichael, *The Last Generation*, 72. On this generation and their educational experiences, also see Stephen William Berry, *All That Makes a Man: Love and Ambition in the Civil War South* (New York: Oxford University Press, 2003); Anya Jabour, *Scarlett's Sisters: Young Women in the Old South* (Chapel Hill: University of North Carolina Press, 2007); Timothy J.

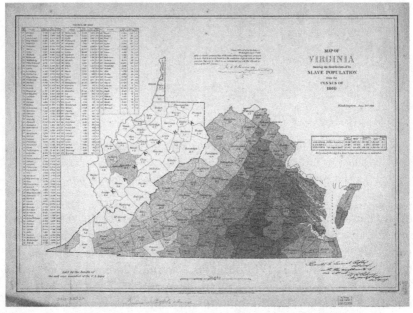

Virginia's slave population based on the 1860 U.S. Census.
Map created by Henry S. Graham, 1861. Library of Congress,
http://hdl.loc.gov/loc.gmd/g3881e.cw1047000

practical, but it did not emphasize extending a young woman's ambition
for success in the way that men's education did. Nevertheless, as female
youth like Mollie read and wrote their way from girlhood to womanhood,
they cultivated personal ambition, questioned social expectations, and
tried to delay marriage as long as possible.[16] Thus, for both young southern men and women like Wash and Mollie, higher education was more
than an education in gentility—it was a means of self-improvement and
an opportunity to rise in social status.

If the Civil War offered an opportunity for young men like Wash Nelson to follow the ambitions for fame and leadership that they cultivated
at school, it was "a personal crisis" for young women like Mollie. Accord-

---

Williams, *Intellectual Manhood: University, Self, and Society in the Antebellum South* (Chapel Hill:
University of North Carolina Press, 2015).

16. Jabour, *Scarlett's Sisters*, 5. Young southern women shared much in common with
northern counterparts when it came to education and intellectual formation. See Mary Kelley, *Learning to Stand & Speak: Women, Education, and Public Life in America's Republic* (Chapel
Hill: University of North Carolina Press, 2006).

ing to the historian Anya Jabour, "The Civil War exacerbated southern girls' discomfort with the status quo by producing tension between customary gender identity (as a southern lady) and a new political identity (as a Confederate rebel)."[17] Yet, the war also presented many new opportunities for young women like Mollie to break through traditional gender expectations and lead their war-torn worlds.[18] In terms of age, the Civil War presented the ultimate, most challenging test for both young men and women on their journeys to adulthood.

It is unclear when Wash and Mollie began courting or became engaged to marry. The letters featured in this collection suggest two possibilities. On the one hand, they may have begun courting before secession and war; if that were the case, the documentary evidence has been lost or destroyed. On the other hand, it is far more likely that the engagement between Wash and Mollie occurred during the war itself, perhaps in the late spring or early summer of 1863, just before the letters in this volume begin. Perhaps Wash visited Mollie as Lee's Army of Northern Virginia moved north in the late spring or early summer of 1863. As a result of this visit, the two may have begun corresponding. The first letter that Mollie sends Wash, for example, indicates that Wash had previously visited her without an official furlough. Was this an intimate meeting? Perhaps. Writing to Wash on April 5, 1864, Mollie reported the engagement of their mutual cousin Fannie and her fiancé, alluding to a room that Wash and Mollie once shared in Middleway. She wrote, "They occupied *our* little room. Those old walls if they could talk could tell some *grand old tales.*"[19] Finally, a letter from April 1865 reveals that Mollie did not know Wash's birthday. If the two had courted for months or years prior to the war, Mollie certainly must have known this detail.[20]

Secession, War, and Capture

Although available letters do not explain Wash's motives for enlisting or clarify his political thought, the voluminous scholarship on why men fought for the Confederacy suggests that the decision to fight was neither

17. Jabour, *Scarlett's Sisters*, 6.

18. Ibid., 240. On Confederate women in public life, see Drew Gilpin Faust, *Mothers of Invention: Women of the Slaveholding South in the American Civil War* (Chapel Hill: University of North Carolina Press, 1996).

19. Mollie to Wash, April 5, 1864, box 2, folder 16, NFP.

20. Mollie to Wash, April 9, 1865, box 2, folder 37, NFP.

automatic nor easy.[21] Peter S. Carmichael has argued that young Virginians of this generation, especially those like Wash, who attended the University of Virginia in the late 1850s, were ambivalent about war. "They loved the Union and abhorred secession," he argues, "but they could not give their allegiance to a national government that did not guarantee Southern rights and political equality."[22] Alongside North Carolinians, Tennesseans, and Arkansans, many Virginians left the Union with reluctance.[23]

In terms of the number of slaves within its borders, the Commonwealth of Virginia was by far the largest and most influential slave state in the Union, and the politics of slavery, particularly the rise of radical abolitionism after Nat Turner's 1831 rebellion in Southampton, Virginia, increased concern that northern fanaticism would erode the state's sovereignty. After briefly considering gradual emancipation and deportation to Africa, the Virginia legislature began reducing the rights of free blacks, tightening "black codes," and digging into the growing defense of slavery.[24] Then, in 1859, the abolitionist John Brown seized the federal arsenal at Harpers Ferry in Jefferson County, Virginia, not far from Mollie Scollay's hometown of Middleway. Given that most Jefferson County residents did not own slaves, Virginia governor Henry A. Wise doubted their fealty to state and region. John Brown's raid proved the power of radical abolitionism and set the stage for Lincoln's election in 1860, which pushed Virginia closer to secession.[25] Just days after Lincoln won the presidency, South Carolina organized a secession convention, and the next month, it seceded; other Deep South states followed, leaving Virginians to decide whether to follow the lower South or remain in the Union.

Virginia and three other states in the upper South were more reluctant to join the Confederacy. They ultimately decided to secede after Confederates fired on Fort Sumter in April 1861, and U.S. President Abraham Lincoln issued a call for volunteers to put down the rebellion. On April 17, 1861, Virginia seceded from the Union, having, according to the Richmond *Dispatch*, "repealed ratification of the Constitution of

21. The most important works on this subject are Berry, *All That Makes a Man*; Carmichael, *The Last Generation*.

22. Carmichael, *The Last Generation*, 119.

23. On young North Carolinians, see Williams, *Intellectual Manhood*, chap. 7.

24. Louis P. Masur, *1831: Year of Eclipse* (New York: Hill and Wang, 2001), 48–62.

25. William A. Link, *Roots of Secession: Slavery and Politics in Antebellum Virginia*, Civil War America (Chapel Hill: University of North Carolina Press, 2005), 217.

the United States of America." On April 25, 1861, the state adopted the Constitution of the Provisional Government of the Confederate States of America. Illustrating the excitement for secession and war, the *Dispatch*'s lead article on April 27, 1861, was a poem by an Alabama author, lauding Virginia's departure from the Union and urging further consolidation of the Confederacy:

> Oh, have you heard the joyful news?
> Virginia does Old Abe refuse,
>> Hurrah, hurrah, hurrah, hurrah.
> Virginia joins the Cotton states,
>> Hurrah, hurrah,
> The glorious cry each heart elates,
>> We'll die for Old Virginia.[26]

War became for many a visceral reaction to perceived northern usurpation and an opportunity to demonstrate the leadership many young men studied and admired in their youth. Over the course of the Civil War, some two hundred thousand white males fought in General Robert E. Lee's Army of Northern Virginia.[27] Approximately fourteen hundred Hanover County men served in the conflict, including those who joined local companies expecting to guard their home counties, as well as conscripts later in the war.[28]

On May 21, 1861, Captain William Nelson organized a battery, and Wash enrolled for service that day at Beaver Dam Depot on the Virginia Central Railroad. The following day Wash was mustered into service in Richmond, just five days before his twenty-first birthday. By February 1862, he had moved up through the ranks from first sergeant to second lieutenant and then captain. On April 30, 1862, he assumed command of, and reorganized, the Hanover Artillery. He was not very popular among the men. "Captain G. W. Nelson and his officers . . . have proved

26. "Hurrah for Old Virginia," *Daily Dispatch* (Richmond, Va.), April 27, 1861.

27. Joseph Glatthaar, "Army of Northern Virginia," *Encyclopedia Virginia*, Virginia Foundation for the Humanities, 2016, accessed April 14, 2017, http://www.encyclopediavirginia .org/Army_of_Northern_Virginia#start_entry 14.

28. This number is based on the names listed on the Confederate war memorial in Hanover County, Va. Bob Krick, National Park Service, e-mail message to Timothy J. Williams, March 3, 2016. The most detailed study of the Army of Northern Virginia is Joseph Glatthaar, *Soldiering in the Army of Northern Virginia: A Statistical Portrait of the Troops Who Served under Robert E. Lee* (Chapel Hill: University of North Carolina Press, 2011). On the Hanover Light Artillery, see Robert H. Moore II, *Miscellaneous Disbanded Virginia Light Artillery* (Lynchburg, Va.: H. E. Howard, Inc., 1997), 117–24.

themselves totally incompetent to command a battery," wrote Private
Henry Robinson Berkeley in July 1862. Blaming Wash for the battery's
disorder, Berkeley wrote, "Wash is as brave a man as I ever saw and fears
nothing, but bravery alone will not keep up a battery. It requires a hard-
working, industrious man of good executive ability; one who never tires,
and is always on the lookout for his men and horses. All of these are
wanting in him [Wash] and his first and second lieutenants."[29] As part of
a major reorganization within Lee's army following the Battle of Antietam, the company disbanded on October 4, 1862, and most of its men
transferred into other companies.[30]

While the artillery was divided between Captain Thomas J. Kirkpat-
rick's Amherst Battery and Captain Pichegru Woolfolk's Hanover County
Battery, Wash was assigned as an artillery officer to General William Nelson Pendleton's staff. According to one of his compatriots, Wash had
met with General Pendleton as soon as he heard about the impending
dissolution of his battery. Apparently, he "came back from Gen. Pendleton's headquarters very well satisfied, having been promised a very soft
place on the General's staff."[31] He commanded a thirty-pound Parrott
gun at the Battle of Fredericksburg in December 1862 and was then assigned the role of inspector of batteries for the First Corps and General
Reserve.[32] During this time, Mollie worried about Wash's whereabouts,
particularly after receiving news of the Battle of Gettysburg (July 1–3,
1863). "We had not been able to hear anything definite from our army
until the receipt of your letter," she wrote on July 7. Indeed, what Wash
experienced in the year between the disbanding of his artillery battery
and his capture and arrest is uncertain. Whatever letters the two exchanged after Gettysburg, if they wrote any at all, are either lost or in
private hands. The letters in this volume nevertheless place Wash in New
Market, Virginia, on October 27, 1863, when he was captured.[33]

Described by a Union artist as "a medley of dilapidated houses with an
inn, a couple of churches, and a town hall," New Market was not far from

---

29. William H. Runge, ed., *Four Years in the Confederate Artillery: The Diary of Private Henry
Robinson Berkeley* (Chapel Hill: Published for the Virginia Historical Society by the University of North Carolina Press, 1961), 23.

30. Ibid., xvi–xviii.

31. Ibid., 31.

32. Ibid., 31n4.

33. Wash's name first appears on a "Descriptive Roll of Prisoners of War at Camp Chase,
Ohio," Service Records. The carded records refer to "Capt. Nelson's Company Virginia
Light Artillery. (Hanover Artillery)."

(Confederate.)

N 1 Hanover arty

Geo. W. Nelson

Cpt. Hanover Arty C S a

Appears on a

List

of Prisoners confined in Military Prison at Wheeling, Va. (also known as Atheneum Prison).

Oct 29/63

Age 23 years; height, 5 ft. 11 in. Complexion florid; eyes blue; hair brown

Occupation

Residence:

Town

County Hanover

State Va

Arrested:

By whom Col Boyd

Where New Market Va

Date Oct 27 , 186 .

Charges

Remarks Sent to Camp Chase Oct 30/63

Reg. No. 96, Dept. West Va., page 121

R W Pearson

(0356) Copyist.

A postwar carded record made from a wartime descriptive list that details Wash Nelson's appearance upon capture. National Archives and Records Administration, Washington, D.C.

Mollie's home in Middleway, where he had met with Mollie a week earlier, perhaps while on furlough following the Battle of Gettysburg.[34] After
visiting Mollie, Wash moved on to New Market and stayed at a "companion's home." While dining, he and his compatriot caught a glimpse
of "a blue coat at the window." Unable to escape, they were captured,
led out of town, and placed under guard the next day. In fact, Wash
carried his first letter written as a prisoner almost to Mollie's doorstep.
Mollie, however, was away in the country and did not receive the letter
containing news of Wash's capture until she returned. Meanwhile, Wash
was transported to Ohio and processed at Camp Chase, a prison established in May 1861 as a Union training camp, located four miles west of
Columbus, Ohio.[35] Two weeks later, Wash departed for Johnson's Island,
a prison for Confederate officers located on a three-hundred-acre island
off the shore of Lake Erie, a little more than two miles from Sandusky,
Ohio, approximately 130 miles from Columbus.[36]

Civil War Prisons and Prisoners

Wash's capture in the fall of 1863 occurred at a crossroads in Civil War
prison policy. When war came in 1861, neither the Union nor the Confederate government had planned on capturing enemy soldiers, let alone
holding large numbers of them in prisons. There simply was no official
protocol, other than precedents set in earlier wars. During the Revolu-
tionary War, captives of a belligerent army were held in prisons rather
than being tried for treason. A more complex exchange system developed during the War of 1812. These prisoners could be traded between
both sides as a form of currency. A captain like Wash Nelson, for example, would have been traded for sixteen privates. This sort of trade allowed both sides to avoid both the human and monetary tolls of holding
prisoners. Importantly, this exchange system depended on the bond of
an oath from paroled prisoners, who promised not take up arms again
until the exchange system evened out the debits and credits.

---

34. James E. Taylor, *With Sheridan up the Shenandoah Valley in 1864: Leaves from a Special
Artist's Sketchbook and Diary* (Cleveland, Ohio: Western Reserve Historical Society, 1989),
444.

35. Roger Pickenpaugh, *Captives in Gray: The Civil War Prisons of the Union* (Tuscaloosa:
University of Alabama Press, 2009), 15.

36. Ibid., 4. See also Roger Pickenpaugh, *Johnson's Island: A Prison for Confederate Officers*
(Kent, Ohio: Kent State University Press, 2016).

This exchange system, a flexible and evolving model, became the default policy during the Civil War. In July 1862, Major General John A. Dix (Union) and Major General Daniel Harvey Hill (Confederate) agreed to a simple policy of prisoner exchange. Once on parole, captured prisoners would be returned to exchange points, on which both sides had previously agreed, within ten days of capture. The policy was humanitarian insofar as it kept prison populations at bay. By May 1863, a combined 32,000 Union and Confederate prisoners had been paroled, and most were officially exchanged. During the first two years of war, a patchwork of individual prisons and ad hoc strategies for operating them fell into place. In the final two years of the war, problems emerged that led to a slow cessation of prisoner exchange.

The first problem involved differing prison conditions. Generally, exchanged Union prisoners came home sicker and weaker than when they had entered confinement, or than Confederate soldiers returning from Union prisons. Union officials began to wonder whether the exchange system benefited the Confederate army more than the Union. The second problem had to do with race and slavery. When Wash and Mollie first began corresponding in early summer, 1863, African American soldiers serving in the Union Army began to see combat and fall into Confederate hands. Confederate officials had previously threatened to turn over black men captured in Union uniforms to state governments so that they could be dealt with under state codes that discouraged slave revolts. Were African Americans, in other words, prisoners of war or insurrectionists? Some Confederates, refusing to acknowledge African Americans' status as soldiers, resorted to executions and thereby threatened the stability of prisoner exchanges altogether. Finally, the third problem was a backlog of Union and Confederate prisoners as both sides sought to create prisons and wage war simultaneously.[37] As a consequence, the prisoner exchange agreement collapsed. Thus, instead of being released within ten days, Wash spent twenty months as a prisoner, beginning with a brief stay at Camp Chase in Ohio and then at Johnson's Island.

Johnson's Island was completed in 1862 and was the only prison built by the Union exclusively for Confederate prisoners, particularly officers. The prison was large, taking up approximately fifteen acres of the three-hundred-acre island. While Wash was imprisoned at Johnson's Island,

---

37. Paul J. Springer and Glenn Robins, *Transforming Civil War Prisons: Lincoln, Lieber, and the Politics of Captivity* (New York: Taylor & Francis, 2015).

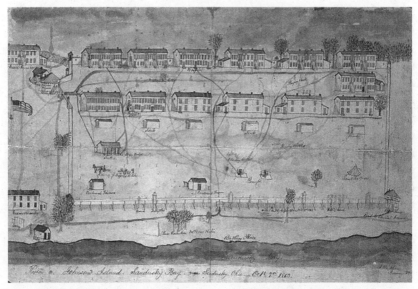

A Confederate prisoner's colored drawing of Johnson's Island, Ohio.
Joseph Mason Kern Papers, #2526-z, Southern Historical Collection,
Wilson Library, University of North Carolina at Chapel Hill.

there were thirteen prison barracks called "blocks" and a sutler's stand
where prisoners could buy supplies, such as food, writing materials, and
clothing.[38]

Prison life was bleak and humiliating. The guards were strict and sometimes abusive. At some Union prisons, black guards watched over Confederates, who vowed never to respect a black man's authority. At places
like Johnson's Island, prisoners were also spectacles for gawking spectators, both male and female. On March 27, 1864, Wash described a bap-
tism of twelve prisoners in the icy waters of Lake Erie, which some local
women had come to observe. "It made me feel very solemn, as I watched
the poor fellows march out into the Lake, loose ice floating on it, singing their hymns, and the guard drawn up on the shore," he wrote. "The
ladies of the Island also graced the occasion with their presence." At John-

---

38. A sutler was a merchant who followed armies during war and sold provisions to soldiers. The checks Wash mentions here were not official currency but the unofficial means
by which sutlers and soldiers carried out transactions. David R Bush, ed., *I Fear I Shall Never
Leave This Island: Life in a Civil War Prison* (Gainesville: University of Florida Press, 2011),
7–8.

son's Island, as well as other prisons, civilians were eager to see prisoners. Entrepreneurs near northern prisons catered to these interests by building observation decks or chartering boats for such voyeurism as Wash described to Mollie.[39]

Material conditions within prisons were poor, if not deadly. There was never enough food, blankets, and clothes, and there were many sources of sickness. Prisoners with family connections in the North received boxes of food and clothing, but this was an infrequent luxury that fostered a two-class system within the prison walls. Those without connections lived on government rations, which varied in quality and quantity. It was not uncommon for prisoners to subsist on spoiled meat, maggot-infested bread, and dirty water. In some instances, hunger produced desperation, and prisoners ate whatever they could stomach. Wash did not experience this degree of suffering until he was moved to Morris Island, South Carolina, and Fort Pulaski, Georgia. In one of the most memorable parts of his memoir, Wash wrote, "Fortunately for some of us—there were a great many cats about the prison and as may be imagined we were glad enough to eat cat. I have been partner in the killing and eating of three, and besides these, friends have frequently given me a share of their cat."[40] Diseases such as scurvy and dysentery resulted from malnutrition in many northern prisons. There were also other forms of hunger and deprivation that gnawed away at prisoners' spirits. Hungering for freedom, for instance, prisoners frequently attempted escape. At Johnson's Island, Wash unsuccessfully attempted to escape twice.

Although few prisoners permanently escaped, religion ameliorated emotional suffering in a number of ways. First, prisoners often held services over which captive clergy presided. Varying in size, these religious services assembled worshipers of many different Christian denominations. Wash wrote about these services in his letters home and made special note when a service was held according to the rituals of the Episcopal Church. Second, prisoners gathered in Bible study and Sunday school classes.[41] Third, prison baptisms, such as those Wash described to Mollie,

---

39. Michael P. Gray, "Captivating Captives: An Excursion to Johnson's Island Civil War Prison," in *The Midwestern Homefront during the Civil War*, ed. Ginette Aley and J. L. Anderson (Carbondale: Southern Illinois University Press, 2013), 16–32; Pickenpaugh, *Captives in Gray*, 100.

40. Nelson, "Memoir."

41. See, for example, "War Diary of Lieut. William Epps," 1864, box 69, folder 43, Military Collection, Civil War Collection, Miscellaneous Records, Reminiscences, etc., State Archives of North Carolina, Raleigh (hereinafter SANC).

also enhanced prisoners' religious lives.[42] Fourth, and perhaps most significantly, prisoners who were more pious, like Wash, maintained private devotional lives through prayer and reading the Bible. Wash's letters contain references to the *Book of Common Prayer* and biblical quotations, as he shared news of his survival and prayers for Mollie's well-being. Of course religious devotion was not for everyone, and sometimes social and spiritual activities clashed. Months before Wash's arrival at Johnson's Island, another devout prisoner complained, "Sunday here does not differ from other days. There is no holy quiet—no holy calm. The same card playing, the same novel reading, the same profanity goes on as other days."[43]

In addition to religion, prisoners maintained as robust a social life as possible. This prison community was even more meaningful when kin and friends found themselves imprisoned together. For example, Wash reported conversations he had with cousins and friends from home. They also attempted to normalize the prison experience. They played card games and told stories; they drank together and smoked pipes, when they were fortunate to receive gifts of liquor (smuggled) and tobacco from home.

Intellectual life also enhanced the friendships forged behind prison walls. Wash wrote, "Our object is to pass time pleasantly and at the same time not to let the mind become a dead letter." Prisoners accomplished this in several ways. They maintained old friendships or forged new ones with fellow captives whose autographs and mailing addresses they gathered into personal journals in order to communicate after the war, if not just to keep the memory of prison life alive. They organized literary clubs, debating societies, and even thespian troupes such as the "Rebel Thespians" at Johnson's Island.[44] In an effort to while away the solitary hours that characterized much of their confinement, they read whatever books and newspapers they could obtain. Johnson's Island Prison, in fact, maintained a borrowing library. Some prisoners also requested books from

---

42. "List of Confederate Prisoner of War Baptisms (1864–1865), Compiled from St. James Records," in Military Collections, SANC.

43. Robert Bingham, August 9, 1863, Diary, in the Robert Bingham Papers, #3731-z, Southern Historical Collection, Wilson Library, University of North Carolina at Chapel Hill (hereinafter SHC). On prison sounds, including noise and religion, see Evan A. Kutzler, "Captive Audiences: Sound, Silence, and Listening in Civil War Prisons," *Journal of Social History* 48, no. 2 (December 2014): 239–63.

44. Pickenpaugh, *Captives in Gray*, 105; John G. Barrett, ed., *Yankee Rebel: The Civil War Journal of Edmund DeWitt Patterson* (Chapel Hill: University of North Carolina Press, 1966), 138; Charles W. Turner, ed. *The Prisoner of War Letters of Lieutenant Thomas Dix Houston (1863–65)* (Verona, Va.: McClure Printing Company, 1980), 15,17.

relatives; others wrote directly to publishers to obtain particular texts for their own amusement.[45] These were the broad contours of prison life that influenced Wash and Mollie's relationship for nearly two years.

A Wartime Courtship

Despite writing to and from prisons in Union-occupied territory, Wash and Mollie were able to forge an intimate bond. Indeed, their courtship rituals resembled those of young couples who, both before and during the war, shared their affections largely through letters.[46] Wash and Mollie did not shy away from writing about their intimate lives and often employed the lofty prose that characterized the Victorian era's epistolary traditions.[47] On March 27, 1864, for example, Wash wrote, "I don't look upon love as simply a 'sweet enchantment' that implies it may be broken, but rather as a soul-filling joy, resting upon & nurtured by the blessed peace of perfect confidence." He frequently declared his love and affection, even as he told Mollie that he spent hours composing poetry using the letters of her name. Just as antebellum youth exchanged locks of hair and tintype photographs, Wash and Mollie also relied on small mementos for consolation. Wash, for example, made a ring for Mollie in prison, which she cherished as a token of his love. Likewise, Wash carried with him certain keepsakes, including a photograph of Mollie. Of course war and imprisonment also uniquely constrained their courtship, particularly in the couple's ability to communicate frequently, freely, and accurately.

Mail was the best means to convey information, but it was not always dependable.[48] Although communication innovations of the late ante-

---

45. Letter from Little, Brown & Co., Publishers and Booksellers, 110 Washington Street, Boston, May 6, 1865, box 1, folder 13, Polk, Brown, and Ewell Family Papers #605, SHC.

46. Victoria E. Ott, *Confederate Daughters: Coming of Age during the Civil War* (Carbondale: Southern Illinois University Press, 2008), 109, 111–12. Ott relied on several excerpted letters from Wash and Mollie that were published in the popular magazine, *Civil War Times Illustrated* 80 (September/October 1995): 28, 73–81; these same excerpts were later republished, see Chris Fordney, ed., "Letters from the Heart," in *The Women's War in the South: Recollections and Reflections of the American Civil War*, ed. Charles G. Waugh and Martin H. Greenberg (Nashville, Tenn.: Cumberland House, 1999), 253–64. On young men, women, and courtship during the Civil War era more broadly, see Berry, *All That Makes a Man*; Jabour, *Scarlett's Sisters*; Williams, *Intellectual Manhood*, chap. 6.

47. Karen Lystra, *Searching the Heart: Women, Men, and Romantic Love in Nineteenth-Century America* (New York: Oxford University Press, 1989).

48. Communication during the Civil War, particularly in the Confederacy, is surprisingly understudied. The most comprehensive work on wartime communication can be found in Jason Phillips, "The Grape Vine Telegraph: Rumors and Confederate Persistence," *Journal*

bellum period—particularly steam printing, railroads, and the telegraph—should have made communication easy in the Confederacy, they
did not. It cost twice as much to mail a letter in the Confederacy as it did
in the United States, and even though the Post Office Department grew
during the war, there were never enough workers to staff it. In addition,
the Confederacy's limited industrial base made paper and stamps ex-
pensive; thus writing, while common, was nevertheless a privilege. Many
southerners used paper scraps for writing letters.[49] Even when supplies
were available, circulation of mail posed another difficulty. Southern mail
routes were centralized around urban hubs, but local postmasters were
unable to work around these routes when circumstances changed, particularly when the Union occupied territories in the South and the newly
formed Union state of West Virginia. In some instances, getting civilian
mail across enemy lines required blockade running. It was easier to send
mail to soldiers than it was to relatives and friends across enemy lines or
within regions. For this reason, the Confederate army operated its own
postal services in lieu of the national post office.[50] According to one history of Jefferson County, a Confederate post office in Shepherdstown
did not last more than a year.[51] Folks on the home front could circum-
vent postal services altogether by sending mail, as Mollie did, by personal
couriers.[52]

The question of privacy was one of the most significant concerns. Mollie's family members usually read correspondence from Wash together
in order to learn of news. Wash's imprisonment added another layer of
complexity. Union and Confederate prisons employed censors to read
all incoming and outgoing mail, and they limited prisoners and their

---

of Southern History 72, no.4 (2006); Phillips, *Diehard Rebels: The Confederate Culture of Invincibility* (Athens: University of Georgia Press, 2007). The history of wartime postal services
of the Union and the Confederacy is also thin. On the Confederacy, see John Nathan
Anderson, "Money or Nothing: Confederate Postal System Collapse during the Civil War,"
American Journalism 30, no. 1 (2013); Yael A. Sternhell, "Communicating War: The Culture
of Information in Richmond during the American Civil War," *Past and Present* 202, no.
1 (2009). On the political uses of mail in particular, see Stephen William Berry, "When
Mail Was Armor: Envelopes of the Great Rebellion, 1861–1865," *Southern Cultures* 4, no. 3
(1998); Steven R. Boyd, *Patriotic Envelopes of the Civil War: The Iconography of Union and Confederate Covers* (Baton Rouge: Louisiana State University Press, 2010).

    49. Anderson, "Money or Nothing," 78, 75.
    50. Ibid., 68, 81, 79.
    51. Bushong, *A History of Jefferson County*, 153.
    52. See Mollie to Wash, envelope, March 13, 1865, box 2, folder 31, NFP. She directed
this letter in care of "L. P. W. Balch."

correspondents to one-page letters.[53] Correspondents nevertheless found ways to work around censors. On March 13, 1865, for example, Wash requested "big paper" and stamps. The former would allow Wash to write more and stick to the one-page limit; the latter were always scarce. Similarly, on April 4, 1865 Mollie wrote, "Write on the blank half sheet that I sent: it is larger than the generality of paper, and you can put more on a page." In addition to manipulating paper size, it was not uncommon for parties to write in coded language. In March 1864, when she wished to report news of the anticipated spring campaign in Virginia, Mollie wrote, "Our boys *at school* are well, and doing well, plenty to *eat* and *wear*. They expect to have a vacation about the first of April, when we hope to see them." Mollie and Wash did not have any children away at school. Instead, she explained that the soldiers from her hometown were doing just fine and either expected a furlough or hoped to be on the move north to recapture northern Virginia in a repeat of spring campaigns in 1862 and 1863.

The idea of censorship upset Mollie, who viewed the act as yet another example of Yankee invasion—deep into her personal life. Throughout the 1850s, white women in Virginia had been taking a more active role in political life by reshaping political questions as extensions of their domestic authority. Yet women guarded their authority over domestic, private matters, which the war first expanded and then eroded.[54] On May 23, 1864, Mollie received a returned letter she had sent to Wash. The letter was marked, "Long letters not delivered. Examiner." Furious at the thought of other eyes reading her letter, she scribbled, "You hateful dog! What business had you writing on my letter." What was, at one level, wartime protocol, appeared on another level to Mollie an invasion of her household and solidified her hatred of the enemy.

In addition to unreliable postal services, lack of privacy, and censorship, prisoners and their loved ones struggled to communicate accurately, given a preponderance of rumor in both printed and oral sources. According to the historian Jason Phillips, "Whether true or false, news traveled far and fast because thousands corresponded with loved ones, Confederate authorities lacked censors and modern propaganda agencies, and a highly partisan media whirled at top speed."[55] Women like Mollie

53. Pickenpaugh, *Captives in Gray*, 98–100.
54. Elizabeth R. Varon, *We Mean to Be Counted: White Women & Politics in Antebellum Virginia* (Chapel Hill: University of North Carolina Press, 1998).
55. Phillips, "The Grape Vine Telegraph," 755.

faced a glut—not a scarcity—of information. However, individual pieces of news or "grape" that came verbally through the "grapevine telegraph" raised suspicions. Unsubstantiated stories from deserters or misinformation from occupying troops flooded social information networks. When Mollie heard accurate news—for example, that the Army of the Potomac had captured Richmond on April 4, 1865—she took it with a grain of salt. Believing either the news was wrong or the setback temporary, Mollie mistook the actual fall of Richmond as rumor rather than reality.

Mollie's location in Jefferson County complicated her experience of "Confederate living." Home to Harpers Ferry Arsenal, Jefferson County was a strategic corridor for both the Union and Confederate armies. Its close proximity to the Baltimore and Ohio Railroad, a crucial supply line, was also significant. By the time of Wash's capture, the county had seen several minor skirmishes, including some associated with Stonewall Jackson's Valley Campaign in the spring of 1862, which brought fighting close to Charles Town. Several times during the war, the Union captured and recaptured nearby Harpers Ferry, and battles occurred in Winchester and Middleway.[56] Moreover, on June 20, 1863, West Virginia was admitted to the Union, and Jefferson County residents divided along Unionist and Confederate lines. Living within the boundaries of this precarious middle ground, Mollie found herself both of and within Virginia and the Confederacy, and of and within West Virginia and the Union.[57]

By January 1864, the Civil War had changed dramatically, bringing greater complications and uncertainties to both Wash and Mollie. It was, quite simply, a discouraging year. Wash again tried escaping from Johnson's Island and, again, failed. Fighting escalated with the brutal and vicious Overland Campaign of 1864, and electoral politics brought the issues of emancipation and African American enlistment to the minds of many soldiers, civilians, and prisoners.[58] Wartime destruction had also

---

56. McPherson, *Battle Cry of Freedom*, 457–58, 648, 777.

57. Bushong, *A History of Jefferson County*, 194–95. The question of West Virginia's statehood—and Jefferson County's inclusion in the new state—was not legally settled until after the war, but the county ultimately became a part of West Virginia.

58. Many scholars point to 1864 as the turning point not only in the Civil War but also in the American experience of war. See Joseph T. Glatthaar, "Battlefield Tactics," and Reid Mitchell, "Not the General but the Soldier: The Study of Civil War Soldiers," in *Writing the Civil War: The Quest to Understand*, ed. James M. McPherson and William J. Cooper Jr. (Columbia: University of South Carolina Press, 1998), 60–80, 81–95. Cultural and environmental historians have also made these claims. See Lisa M. Brady, *War upon the Land: Military Strategy and the Transformation of Southern Landscapes during the American Civil War* (Athens: University of Georgia Press, 2012), esp. chaps. 3 and 4; Megan Kate Nelson, *Ruin*

A map of Virginia in 1861, showing Jefferson County, Hanover County,
important rail lines, and Point Lookout, Maryland. J. W. Randolph, *New Map
of Virginia, compiled from the latest Maps. 1861.* Library of Congress, Geography
and Map Division, http://hdl.loc.gov/loc.ndlpcoop/glva01.lva00089.

become increasingly visible in popular culture by 1864. Photographs
and drawings of wounded and dead soldiers—as well as sick and frail
prisoners—circulated widely in Union and Confederate newspapers and
magazines.[59] According to the historian Benjamin Cloyd, a "steady publication of articles, pictures, cartoons, prisoner testimony, and even government reports" of conditions in Union prisons circulated within the
Confederacy.[60] The degraded conditions in both Union and Confederate prisons resulted from the cessation of prisoner exchanges in 1863.

Nation: Destruction and the American Civil War, UnCivil Wars (Athens: University of Georgia
Press, 2012).

59. This first occurred in 1862, with Gardner's photos of Antietam, and most famously
in 1863 with Brady's photos of Gettysburg. See Nelson, *Ruin Nation,* 167.

60. Cloyd, *Haunted by Atrocity,* 31. In the Union, the most popular images were Thomas
Nast's drawings, which appeared in wartime runs of *Harper's Weekly.*

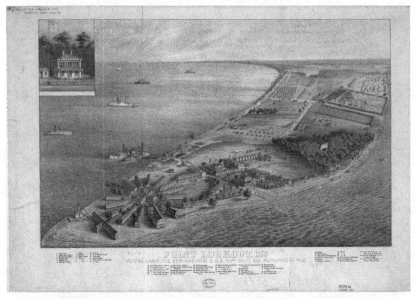

This bird's-eye view drawing of Point Lookout, Maryland, depicts
Hammond General Hospital and the prison for Confederate soldiers.
Library of Congress, http://hdl.loc.gov/loc.pnp/pga.02593.

When it became clear that the Confederacy refused to treat black soldiers as legitimate prisoners of war, prisoner exchanges slowed nearly to
a halt.[61] With far more prisoners entering prisons than leaving through
exchange, prisons became sites of deadly famine and pestilence, provoking public outcry. Wash and Mollie were likely aware of the wider public
debate about prisoner treatment but underestimated its effect on the
prospect of a speedy exchange.

For Wash, the year of 1864 was also one of considerable travel. In April
1864, he was sent from Johnson's Island to Point Lookout, Maryland.
First opened in July 1863 on the peninsula jutting out into the meeting
of the Potomac River and the Chesapeake Bay, Point Lookout eventually held more than twenty thousand prisoners.[62] A week after moving to
Point Lookout, Wash came down with chronic dysentery and was admitted to the Hammond USA General Hospital, adjacent to the prison. He
recovered, and two months later, in June, Wash was transferred to Fort

61. Ibid., 8.
62. Lonnie R. Speer, *Portals to Hell: Military Prisons of the Civil War* (Mechanicsburg, Pa:
Stackpole Books, 1997), 151–52.

The empty stockade on Morris Island, site of Wash's
imprisonment in 1864, near Battery Wagner, where the
African American 54th Massachusetts fought the previous
year. Morris Island, South Carolina, stockade, 1865, Library of
Congress, https://www.loc.gov/itemcwp2003005334/PP/.

Delaware, a river fortification on Pea Patch Island in the middle of the
Delaware River separating Delaware and New Jersey. Active for much of
the war, after 1863 the site became heavily used as a prison for Confederates. Here, Wash spent his time practicing gymnastics (which worried
Mollie greatly), reading, and talking with other prisoners, from whom he
heard rumors of yet another prison transfer. In late summer, he and his
fellow officers were taken to Morris Island, South Carolina, and placed
near a Union artillery battery and in range of the Confederate guns

defending Charleston in retaliation for similar treatment of Union officers by Confederates inside the besieged city.[63] In these ways, the stage
was set for both Mollie and Wash to turn inward to contemplate who they
were as a couple and as individuals.

Gender in Crisis

As Mollie remained at home in Middleway, war, separation, and Yankee
occupation jolted her experiences of and attitudes about womanhood.
In terms of work, southern women's responsibilities increased in the absence of able-bodied males and slaves.[64] Mollie complained of having
to perform "slave work" such as cooking and cleaning. In addition to
maintaining their homes and farms, Mollie and her female friends and
cousins also tended their communities' needs by teaching school and
Sunday school. These and other tasks were unique to wartime. Women
in Mollie's social world also prepared graves and memorials for fallen
soldiers and played an important role in tacitly assuring prisoners' emotional stability by writing letters to many prisoners, even if they did not
personally know them. On March 21, 1865, Mollie wrote to Wash at Fort
Delaware, "I have been corresponding all winter with a soldier at Fort
Del . . . you can make his acquaintance if you choose, and let me know
what you think of him. As he is a stranger to me, I am unable to give any
opinion." Later that year she admitted to not being able to take on additional letter writing projects for want of time and energy.

Importantly, class standing enhanced Mollie's experiences of war. The
consistently declining Virginia economy propelled hundreds of women

---

63. Wartime laws established by Francis Lieber's General Order's No. 100 called for
the use of careful retaliation as a way to bind belligerents to a set of principles and curtail
human losses. This group of officers selected for retaliation contributed to postwar debates
about treatment of prisoners and became lionized in Lost Cause histories of the conflict. In
1905, for example, J. Ogden Murray published *The Immortal Six Hundred: A Story of Cruelty to
Confederate Prisoners of War*, dedicating the work to his fellow Confederate officers confined
"under fire of our own guns" on Morris Island, S.C., and at Fort Pulaski "on rations of rotten
corn meal and pickle." According to Murray, the book was not only to describe a tale of
heroic suffering but also to provide a history "of the wanton cruelty inflicted upon helpless
prisoners of war, without the least shadow of excuse." John Ogden Murray, *The Immortal Six
Hundred: A Story of Cruelty to Confederate Prisoners of War* (Winchester, Va.: Eddy Press Corp.,
1905), 9. For an earlier example, see Fritz Fuzzlebug, *Prison Life during the Rebellion; Being
a Brief Narrative of the Miseries and Sufferings of Six Hundred Confederate Prisoners Sent from Fort
Delaware to Morris' Island to be Punished* (Singer's Glen, Va.: J. Funk's Sons, printers, 1869).

64. Faust, *Mothers of Invention*, 74–79; LeeAnn Whites, "The Civil War as a Crisis in Gender," in *Divided Houses: Gender and the Civil War*, ed. Catherine Clinton and Nina Silber (New
York: Oxford University Press, 1992).

into bread lines in Richmond, but not Mollie. In fact, she attended picnics and family gatherings, where she enjoyed feasts that she hesitated even mentioning to Wash. This was typical of her social class. According to the historian Anne Sarah Rubin, there was a "dichotomy between suffering and socializing" in Richmond, where many elite women, "unwilling to live a life without intellectual and social stimulation," attended balls, parties, and picnics. In doing so, they broke the monotony of war.[65]

Not surprisingly, race further complicated Mollie's experiences as a woman on the southern home front. After the Union army began to enlist African Americans, Mollie feared that armed blacks would incite large-scale massacres. On April 5, 1864, Mollie told Wash that a black regiment had been near Winchester, Virginia, and was headed north to Charles Town. "I trust they will not get here," she wrote. "I have the greatest horror of them." She was particularly appalled that Union officers had begun enlisting black men from Jefferson County. "It was galling to the flesh I assure you, but this is only one of the numerous indignations, to which we are every day subjected; however we bear it all cheerfully as it is for the good of our Confederacy."[66]

As historians have argued, war also influenced how men like Wash Nelson thought about themselves *as men*. This had less to do with issues of work and responsibility and more to do with honor and character. The simplest way to view honor is as a concept somewhat synonymous with reputation. If a man's reputation was besmirched in the eyes of his equals, his peers, then he would seek to vindicate the injustice, with violence if necessary.[67] In terms of Confederates, one historian has argued that honor was "the lingua franca of southern sectionalism." Southerners believed that northern antislavery politics threatened their group sense of honor and they vindicated their honor with secession.[68]

Several developments in the fall of 1864 and the winter of 1865 brought about Wash's concerns with manhood, including his sense of honor. Most fundamentally, during these years, letters to and from Mol-

---

65. Anne S. Rubin, *A Shattered Nation: The Rise and Fall of the Confederacy, 1861–1868*, Civil War America (Chapel Hill: University of North Carolina Press, 2005), 67–68.

66. Mollie to Wash, April 5, 1864, box 2, folder 16, NFP.

67. Bertram Wyatt-Brown, *The Shaping of Southern Culture: Honor, Grace, and War, 1760s–1890s* (Chapel Hill: University of North Carolina Press, 2001); Wyatt-Brown, *Southern Honor: Ethics and Behavior in the Old South* (New York: Oxford University Press, 1982); John Mayfield and Todd Hagstette, eds., *The Field of Honor: Essays on Southern Character and American Identity* (Columbia: University of South Carolina Press, 2017), xix–xx.

68. Christopher J. Olsen, *Political Culture and Secession in Mississippi: Masculinity, Honor, and the Antiparty Tradition, 1830–1860* (Oxford, England: Oxford University Press, 2000), 9.

lie slowed nearly to a halt, and Wash turned inward to examine his own life. In the spring of 1865, Wash Nelson turned twenty-five years old. Although he was at the prime of his manhood, he felt like a caged tiger and believed he looked like an "old looking young man." Visible changes in his body and appearance alarmed him. He feared that any gentility he possessed before the war had disappeared; he feared returning from war a lesser man than when he entered.

Wash's anxiety about his haggard looks and poor clothing reflects an important cultural continuity in the Civil War era, as elite whites believed public presentation was paramount in conveying honor and reputation.[69] The Civil War had postponed his professional goals and his love life, and he worried this would ultimately harm his relationship with Mollie and prevent their marriage. Moreover, as rumors circulated in prison about Lee's surrender at Appomattox, Wash faced the ultimate embarrassment of swearing an oath of allegiance to the United States. For many southern men, admitting defeat and swearing the oath of allegiance were the ultimate expressions of dishonor and constituted emasculation.

In addition to the dishonor of defeat, Wash questioned whether Mollie would still love him if he swore fealty to the Union. While Mollie had a strong voice throughout their relationship, her assertiveness may have become more important in the final months of the war. In April 1865, Mollie wrote that she hoped Wash handled the news of Richmond's capture "as philosophically as I did."[70] Shortly thereafter, Wash felt compelled to justify to Mollie his taking the oath of allegiance. Wash explained that he and fellow officers held a meeting and came to the conclusion that because the Confederate government no longer existed "our obligations to it were at an end, and our honor could no way be compromised by any course we might pursue with regard to it." However, he still worried how this would sound to Mollie's ears, "that by a false step now I might lose you forever. . . . If you love me write immediately."[71] Although Mollie reassured Wash that she approved of his decision, Wash had the cultural predisposition to believe that her love was conditional upon his honor.

Race, too, played an important role in Wash's conception of manhood. Sometimes the first armed black men whom Confederate prisoners saw

---

69. Kenneth S. Greenberg, *Honor & Slavery: Lies, Duels, Noses, Masks, Dressing as a Woman, Gifts, Strangers, Humanitarianism, Death, Slave Rebellions, the Proslavery Argument, Baseball, Hunting, and Gambling in the Old South* (Princeton, N.J.: Princeton University Press, 1996).

70. Mollie to Wash, April 9, 1865, box 2, folder 37, NFP.

71. Wash to Mollie, May 3, 1865, box 2, folder 42, NFP.

were their guards at prisons such as Point Lookout or Morris Island.[72] For them, being guarded by black soldiers became an important indignity. At Point Lookout Prison, the Confederate artist John Jacob Omenhausser drew a scene in which a black soldier standing on a walkway alongside the prison fence looks down upon a suppliant white prisoner. The caption, written in racialized dialect, states "Sentinel: Git away from dat dar fence white man, or I'll make old Abe's gun smoke at you. I can hardly hold de ball back now. De bottom rails on top now."[73] While perhaps apocryphal, that last sentence came to exemplify conservative southerners' fears of black agency for years to come.

Fears of the alliance between African Americans, the Union army, and the U.S. government simmered in Wash's memoir.[74] At Morris Island and Fort Pulaski, Wash Nelson described African American guards as "uncouth and barbarous," as well as trigger happy. Still, he also described them as preferable to the white men who associated with them as their officers. Drawing from racialized medical theories, Wash wrote in his memoir, "If physiognomy be any index of character, then certainly those officers were villainous." This racialist thought, which came to define the postwar South, crystallized for Wash in prison.

On June 13, 1865—just two months after Lee's surrender to Grant at Appomattox Courthouse—Wash took the oath of allegiance and was released from Fort Delaware. In the following months he readjusted to civilian life and made preparations with Mollie for their upcoming nuptials. Between June and October, the couple was both excited and anxious. With black slaves now free persons, occupying Union soldiers, and Reconstruction looming large, Wash looked to marriage to reassert whatever claims to authority and patriarchy he might have had before the war. These tensions are palpable in some of the last letters in this collection. In a postwar letter, Wash referenced Mollie's intention to act "'as willful as possible.'" He replied he would wait until marriage before getting out his Bible and showing her where it says, "wife obey your husband."[75] It

72. Early slave laws prohibited male slaves from possessing firearms. Thomas D. Morris, *Southern Slavery and the Law, 1619–1860* (Chapel Hill: University of North Carolina Press, 1996), 266.

73. John Jacob Omenhausser, Civil War sketchbook, Point Lookout, Md., 1864–1865, Maryland Manuscript #5213, Maryland Manuscripts Collection, Special Collections, University of Maryland at College Park Libraries.

74. On this alliance, see Chandra Manning, *Troubled Refuge: Struggling for Freedom during the Civil War* (New York: Alfred A. Knopf, 2016), 12–25.

75. Wash to Mollie, September 4, 1865, box 3, folder 10, NFP.

"De bottom rails on top now." Dialogue between a black guard and a prisoner, revealing the racial tension between prisoners and black guards. John Jacob Omenhausser, Civil War sketchbook, Point Lookout, Md., 1864–1865, Maryland Manuscript #5213, Maryland Manuscripts Collection, Special Collections, University of Maryland at College Park Libraries.

was a joke, a veiled threat, or somewhere in the middle. At times Mollie encouraged this sort of dialogue, telling Wash, "I would not marry a man unless he were my superior. I should not respect him and how could I love one whom I did not respect."[76] Other lines hinted at Wash's own

---

76. Mollie to Wash, September 25, 1865, box 3, folder 9, NFP.

fragility. Mollie had stated earlier her intention not to talk about the wedding until he arrived at her home. Wash did not push the issue, but he suggested that it must be too delightful a subject for her to write about. "Only let me love you," he wrote, "and love me a little in return, and I will be as pliant as clay."[77]

Wash and Mollie married on October 17, 1865, in Virginia. Not long thereafter, Wash was ordained an Episcopal priest, like his father before him. Between 1880 and his death in 1903, Wash served as rector of St. James Episcopal Church in Warrenton, a town located in Fauquier County, Virginia.[78] He resigned on account of "long-continued illness" in May 1903 and died the next month. He is buried at the Warrenton Cemetery.[79] Over the course of their thirty-four-year marriage, Wash and Mollie had nine children, eight of whom survived them.[80]

Wash's Memoir and the Lost Cause

In 1866, Wash drafted a memoir, which appears at the end of this volume. Wash never explained why he wrote a memoir. In many ways, though, writing a memoir might have satisfied Wash's emotional need for closure and catharsis, or at the very least to consolidate the memory of the most painful experiences of his life. After all, prisoners of war faced more than just shot and shell, and they worried that stories of battlefield glory would overshadow their experiences of physical and mental suffering. They also passed through experiences that proved to be more difficult to reconcile. In the immediate postwar years, northerners and southerners began to write extensively about their personal experiences, which in turn generated sectional debates about each side's culpability for wartime atrocities. The writings of prisoners were some of the most controversial.[81]

Settling the prisoner treatment question had much to do with preserving southern honor—an issue with which Wash struggled during

77. Wash to Mollie, September 4, 1865, box 3, folder 10, NFP.

78. A. N. Brockway, ed., *Catalogue of the Delta Kappa Epsilon Fraternity* (New York: Council Publishing Company, 1900), 179.

79. *Alexandria Gazette*, Alexandria, Va., May 30, 1903, 3, and June 1, 1903, 2.

80. Harris, *Harris Family*, 80. Their fourth child, Jane Crease Nelson died in infancy (December 15, 1873–December 19, 1873).

81. The postwar readjustment of Confederate veterans to society has recently garnered much scholarly attention. Some exemplary works include Gaines M. Foster, *Ghosts of the Confederacy: Defeat, the Lost Cause, and the Emergency of the New South, 1865 to 1913* (New York: Oxford University Press, 1987); M. Keith Harris, *Across the Bloody Chasm: The Culture of Commemoration among Civil War Veterans* (Baton Rouge: Louisiana State University Press, 2014); Nelson, *Ruin Nation*.

Rev. George Washington Nelson Jr. (1840–1903) photographed in clerical
collar ca. 1895. Nelson Family Collection, Catalog No. 1980.00114.080,
Clarke County Historical Association Archives, Berryville, Va.

nearly two years of imprisonment and even more so when he returned home, with the bitter taste of pledging allegiance to the Union still on his tongue, and with the prospect of facing former slaves as free men and women. In September 1865, for example, he mentioned in a letter a confrontation with a "negro boy." His summary of the encounter reveals his sense of racial superiority characteristic of the postwar era: "I had a good deal of trouble [with the "negro boy"]. It was the worse for him though, as I had to knock him down, and I hit a pretty hard lick." Wash also indicated that the boy's parents seemed ready to intervene but he "advised them not, as I should certainly kill them if they did, and they took my advice."[82] Such a violent outburst, coming from someone planning to become a minister, demonstrates how Wash's worldview connected masculine honor with racial superiority. Furthermore, this casual flirtation with violence within Wash's letter offers an early illustration of the racial violence that characterized militant white resistance during Reconstruction. Postwar narratives were forged in this context of dishonor, bitterness, resentment, and white supremacy, especially those about the experiences of Union and Confederate prisoners.

Prison narratives became ubiquitous in postwar American print culture, with new works appearing well into the early twentieth century. First-hand accounts of Union and Confederate prisons came into print as books, as well as articles, reminiscences, and poetry, in magazines, such as the *Southern Historical Society Papers* (*SHSP*) and the more popular and longer-lived *Confederate Veteran*.[83] In March 1876, the *SHSP* published its third issue, which was devoted entirely to the treatment of Confederate prisoners during the Civil War. The editor wrote, "There is, perhaps no subject connected with the late war which more imperatively demands discussion at our hands than the *Prison Question*." He reminded his readers that the northern media had agitated this discussion during the war

---

82. Wash to Mollie, September 4, 1865, box 3, folder 9, NFP.

83. Hesseltine, *Civil War Prisons*, 247–48. In fact, perhaps because of this outpouring of material, publishers adapted the term "deadline," which once referred to a feature of prison camps, into their own professional jargon. Scholars interested in the Lost Cause and historical memory of the Civil War have mostly focused on postwar sources such as the *Southern Historical Society Papers* and the more popular and longer-lived *Confederate Veteran*. Ray M. Atchison, "'The Land We Love': A Southern Post-Bellum Magazine of Agriculture, Literature, and Military History," *North Carolina Historical Review* 37, no. 4 (1960); Steven E. Sodergren, "'The Great Weight of Responsibility': The Struggle over History and Memory in Confederate Veteran Magazine," *Southern Cultures* 19, no. 3 (2013); Richard D. Starnes, "Forever Faithful: The Southern Historical Society and Confederate Historical Memory," *Southern Cultures* 2, no. 2 (1996).

years, reporting "Rebel barbarities" against Union soldiers imprisoned in Confederate prisons. It was time, he argued, to correct the record.[84] Popular magazines played an important role in coming to terms with defeat by preserving war records and memoirs, as well as disseminating uniquely "southern" histories of the war. Magazine editors contributed historical sketches of battles and veritable hagiographies of the Confederacy's most laureled leaders.

Wash's memoir reflects an early influence in Lost Cause literature. Confederate officers took the lead in replying to northern critics of southern prisons. These memoirs focused on the survival of southern officers under the harsh rule of Union prison keepers. Wash also held an influential role as a member of the so-called Immortal Six Hundred. This group gained the sobriquet when the officers were moved from northern prisons to Morris Island, South Carolina, placed within range of Confederate artillery, and reportedly given rations comparable to Union soldiers at Andersonville. Most of them were slaveholders or came from slaveholding families, and they had opportunities to improve their minds through education and professional training in the years before the Civil War. The social standing of officers meant that they were more likely to keep journals or write letters during their service. They were also much more likely to write for publication after the war had ended. Wash hints at this in the 1866 manuscript: "It is my intention to give full credit for every kindness, for stretched to the utmost, they are but two or three bright spots in a dark record of suffering and oppression." After ten months, his indignation was still very fresh.

Wash's identity as an Episcopalian is also significant in the broader story of the Lost Cause. According to the historian Charles Reagan Wilson, the Lost Cause operated as a type of "civil religion" that appealed to Protestant southerners, in particular. Wilson argues, "While Methodists and Baptists openly endorsed and participated in the religious atmosphere of the Lost Cause rituals, the Episcopalians played an especially prominent role in the Southern civil religion, particularly in its rituals." Wilson notes that "The army's leadership was laced with Episcopalians, including Lee, Leonidas Polk, and Ellis Capers." This also applied to lower-ranking officers, such as Wash Nelson, whose prison letters hinted

---

84. "The Treatment of Prisoners During the War between the States," *Southern Historical Society Papers*, 1, no. 3 (March 1876): 113.

at the importance of the denomination's particular liturgies, played an important role in this process.[85]

While the documents contained in this volume do not demonstrate Wash's role as a clergyman in any Lost Cause commemorative ceremonies, his memoir foreshadows the Lost Cause school of Civil War historiography. It also contrasts sharply with his correspondence with Mollie. The letters document intimate experiences created and shared by men and women, while the memoir is largely a man's testimony to prison life. The striking distinction between the letters and the memoir is that while the former is a romance between a man and a woman, the latter is a drama between a man and his male captors. When Wash's sister, Jennie, copied the memoir in 1866 she recorded, quite disappointed, that he chose not to mention the prison letters. "Some of the most touching incidents of his prison life were in connection with his letters," she wrote, "to which—naturally he does not choose to refer." Perhaps, after having lost a war, it would have been further emasculating for Wash to admit that his source of strength throughout the conflict had been from his fiancée.

In these ways, the documents that follow contribute to, and invite consideration of, a broader historiographical concern with postwar psychology and the construction of the "Lost Cause." Some historical works have called attention to the unique role of Civil War prisons and prisoners in the broader cultural process of retrenchment and reunion, but the full impact of this relationship has not received due attention. In one of only a few caveats in his groundbreaking work of synthesis, *Race and Reunion* (2002), David Blight points out that the physical and emotional wounds of captivity never healed in the Civil War generation. Furthermore, Caroline Janney and William Blair suggest that debates about treatment of prisoners kept wounds open among this generation. Janney indicates that by the 1870s, former Confederates went on the offensive, arguing that Confederate prisoners had suffered worse than Union prisoners.[86] In his foreword to a reprinting of William Hesseltine's early overview

---

85. Charles Reagan Wilson, *Baptized in Blood: The Religion of the Lost Cause, 1865–1920* (Athens: University of Georgia Press), 35–36. On Leonidas Polk, in particular, see Glenn Robins, *The Bishop of the Old South: The Ministry and Civil War Legacy of Leonidas Polk* (Macon, Ga.: Mercer University Press, 2006), 198–99, 202–15.

86. David W. Blight, *Race and Reunion: The Civil War in American Memory* (Cambridge, Mass.: Belknap Press of Harvard University Press, 2001), 152–53; Caroline E. Janney, *Remembering the Civil War: Reunion and the Limits of Reconstruction* (Chapel Hill: University of North Carolina Pres, 2013), 151–52.

of Civil War prisons, Blair urges historians to examine the intricacies of how wartime trauma in prison, public debate over treatment, and Civil War memory related in the postwar South. Still, the only scholarly work to examine this larger historical problem about reunion and memory is Benjamin Cloyd's study, *Haunted by Atrocity*. His work on the afterlife of Civil War prisons highlights the persistent uncertainty about the meaning of captivity and atrocity in the 150 years after the Civil War, and opens the field to more nuanced work on the social, cultural, and even gendered significance of these institutions.[87]

Considered together, the memoir and wartime letters provide a window into prison life that students and scholars rarely see together. The letters were semiprivate, while the memoir was intended—like so many other Confederate reminiscences—to offer public testimony to perceived injustice and trauma. This volume, therefore, offers exciting opportunities for analysis and future research. In particular, it poses three related questions about history: What role does memory play in culture? How can historians reconstruct and interpret the past given conflicting sources based on memories? How did memory influence the recording, writing, and rewriting of the Confederate past? By juxtaposing the letters and memoir in a single volume, this book shows the generation and regeneration of wartime memory and history at work.

---

87. William Blair, foreword to Hesseltine, *Civil War Prisons*, xvii–xx; Cloyd, *Haunted by Atrocity* (Baton Rouge: Louisiana State University Press, 2010).

Editorial Method

This volume presents the entire collection of fifty-five extant letters that George Washington Nelson Jr. (Wash) and his fiancée, Mary Scollay (Mollie), exchanged between 1863 and 1865. They are housed in the Nelson Family Papers collection at Virginia Tech's Special Collections Library (Blacksburg, Va.); copies are also held at Long Branch Plantation (Millwood, Va.). There are five letters from 1863, twenty-six from 1864, and twenty-four from 1865. Envelopes for many of these letters exist in the collection, and they have helped track the movement of correspondence. To our knowledge, extant letters from the period 1867–71 either do not exist or are untraceable. There are only four letters from the period 1871–72, but because none of them furthers the narrative that the wartime letters present, we have not included them here.

The letters in this volume vary in length, sometimes numbering as many as five handwritten pages, but most do not exceed one handwritten page. This brevity was a requirement of prison censors, who set this page limit for letters entering and exiting prisons in order facilitate timely delivery. Longer letters took additional time for censors to scrutinize and were often delayed, causing anxiety for both Wash and Mollie. Not all letters arrived when planned, and sometimes Mollie and Wash received multiple letters at once. Other times, letters never arrived. As a result, there are letters missing from this collection.

In addition to the letters, this volume also features Wash's 1866 memoir. Two versions of the memoir are held at the Virginia Historical Society (Richmond, Va.): an undated typed transcript, probably from the mid-twentieth century, and a manuscript in the hand of Wash's sister, Jennie, dated 1866. It is unknown whether Wash dictated his reminiscences, and this is the only copy of the memoir, or whether Jenny penned a copy for herself later that year, and Wash's original draft is in private hands or lost. The physical condition of Jennie's manuscript copy suggests, however, that the latter case is more likely, as these pages seem to have been pasted into an album at one time. Significantly, when Jenny copied the narrative, she remarked how she "wanted Wash to rewrite this, condensing a little and adding other items of great interest—but he says he can't." She wrote further, "Some of the most touching incidents of his prison life were in connection with his letters—to which—naturally he does not choose to refer." Jennie reminds us that all historical narratives require choice and are never complete.

In March 1876, Wash's memoir was published in an issue of the *Southern Historical Society Papers* devoted entirely to treatment of Confederate prisoners of war. Created by the Southern Historical Society in 1873, the *SHSP* was intended to promote a distinctly southern history of the Civil War. The publication circulated fairly widely among Confederate veterans, though it never reached the popularity of the more familiar *Confederate Veteran*. Regarding Wash's memoir in particular, the editor wrote, "The narrative was written not long after the close of the war, when the facts were fresh in his memory, and could be substantiated by memoranda in his possession." Apparently, Wash wrote to the editor that his reminiscences were "all literal fact, *understated rather than overstated*." Wash also explained that he shared the story with his fellow bunkmate while at Point Lookout, who corroborated Wash's facts.[1]

We have retranscribed the memoir from the original manuscript and provided scholarly annotations for pertinent historical terms and proper nouns, as well as unfamiliar language. Our annotated version of Wash's memoir is significant for many reasons, but especially because it removes it from a politically oriented Lost Cause rendering of the Civil War found in the *SHSP*, placing it, instead, within the context of Wash and Mollie's lived experiences of war and defeat. In transcribing the memoir for this volume, we worked from both the typed transcript and Jenny's 1866 manuscript, as well as the version published in the *Southern Historical Society Papers*. In many cases, the typed transcript was inaccurate, and we have corrected those errors. The version in the *SHSP* does not always follow the original manuscript's paragraph breaks and, as a result, is less accessible for students and researchers.

We transcribed both the letters and memoir using high-resolution digital images of the original manuscripts, though we each worked with the physical materials in the archives as well. In order not to encumber the reading of these sources, we have retained original spelling without the use of [*sic*], unless doing so offered needed clarification. In instances when either writer repeated a word or phrase in succession, we deleted the repeated word. We have also omitted phrases that the au-

---

1. *Southern Historical Society Papers* 1, no. 3 (March 1876): 243.

thors struck in the original manuscript. Biblical quotations in the letters came from the King James Version of the Bible, which was the only version Wash and Mollie would have known. Finally, we took certain editorial liberties with style, formatting, and punctuation. We silently indented paragraphs where they broke and capitalized the first words of sentences when the authors did not. Too, Wash and Mollie often ended sentences with dashes, and we replaced them with periods. In the case of possessive nouns, Wash placed apostrophes over the penultimate letter, but we have transcribed the word according to modern conventions. Similarly, we have removed superscripts for ordinal numbers and also standardized the alignment for the openings, closings, and dates of the letters. Finally, although Wash's sister signed the manuscript memoir, "Jenny," both Wash and Mollie spelled her name "Jennie" in their correspondence, and so did we.

We have identified the most significant personal and place names, as well as battles, that appear in each letter. In some cases, we have not identified individuals with minor significance to the broader narrative; often these family acquaintances or friends were impossible to locate in the historical record with the information available in the letters. In identifying many individuals from the Nelson and Page families, we consulted Richard Channing Moore's *Genealogy of the Page Family in Virginia* (1893). For other individuals, we relied on digital images of U.S. census records from the Library of Congress microfilm collection of these records that are held in databases on *Ancestry.com* (http://www.ancestry.com). We also used this website to corroborate information in Moore's *Genealogy*. In order to render our annotations in a clear and useful way, we have only cited the permanent census information: microfilm collection information and pertinent page, dwelling, and family numbers. Readers should note that we accessed all census material on *Ancestry.com*. We have also taken care to gloss Latin and French phrases, and annotate literary extracts. Doing so underscores the broader intellectual culture of the Civil War era from which Wash and Mollie drew inspiration.

CHAPTER 1

1863

From Soldier to Prisoner

Wash Nelson had been off fighting for the Confederacy, communicating with Mollie intermittently. He had recently visited with her at her home in northern Virginia, though the circumstances of his absence from the army are unclear because the sources do not refer to an official furlough or pass. Perhaps Wash took advantage of his position on General William Nelson Pendleton's staff and surprised Mollie with a visit without leave. Because Wash's command moved frequently, Mollie often did not know where to direct her letters and was usually anxious about her fiancé's whereabouts. In the following letters, Wash reassured Mollie of his safety and reported news about the war, his capture, and imprisonment. Mollie returned news of family and friends. Wash wrote to Mollie nearly immediately after his capture, and the letters that follow his capture begin the central story of this collection.

"Home"[1] July 6, 1863

My Dear Wash

Your kind and interesting letter gave me much pleasure, and although I do not know of any way to send you an answer I will write, hoping that Providence may soon favor me with an opportunity. We had not been able to hear anything definite from our army until the receipt of your letter. Of course reports of all kinds both good and bad are current, the latter of which I generally try not to believe.

---

1. Middleway, Jefferson County, Va.

Yesterday evening we heard that a severe fight had taken place near Gettysburg[2] in which we had been rather unsuccessful losing ten thousand men[3] &c &c.

I sincerely hope this report may not be true. Though I do not doubt there has been a fight, still I hope it has pleased a kind Providence again "to bless our arms with victory."

What would we do in this world without hope? If I had been told when our army went out last fall that we were to be under Yankee rule until June I think I could scarcely have lived through the Winter, but as it was, though often cast down by repeated disappointments, still we hoped that each day would bring us some news of the approach of our army, and in this way we managed to get through the long, long Winter and Spring. I fear it will be sometime before we can hear any reliable news from the fight.

Please write as soon as you can, and tell us all about it. O! How it would grieve me to know that any of my dear relations had to be buried upon Yankee soil. Remember Wash if you get wounded, you are to come to Smithfield.[4]

Our cousin Jefferson Page[5] left here on Thursday, having spent the night before with us. We feel anxious to hear how he stood the trip, for we did not think him well enough to go, though he seemed so anxious to get on to his command that our persuasions did not have much effect. We all fell desperately in love with our new cousin, indeed I don't know that I ever saw anyone with whom I was more pleased, upon such a short acquaintance. Well! How do you like Yankee land upon further acquaintance? I am afraid you will all be so much pleased with the nice *eating* over there, you will not be able to stand confederate living. What do you

---

2. The Battle of Gettysburg, Pa., took place on July 1–3, 1863.

3. Mollie reports ten thousand Confederate casualties. In actuality, the Confederacy lost nearly twenty-eight thousand men. James McPherson, *Battle Cry of Freedom: The Civil War Era* (Oxford, England: Oxford University Press, 1988), 664.

4. Smithfield was the earlier name for the town that became Middleway. Another historic name for the town was "Wizard Clip," which Mollie references in a letter to Wash on January 16, 1864 (see chap. 2). Middleway Historic District, Jefferson County, W.Va., Nomination to the National Register of Historic Places, 1973, on *West Virginia Division of Culture and History* website, http://www.wvculture.org/shpo/nr/pdf/jefferson/80004025.pdf

5. Possibly Thomas Jefferson Page (1808–99), who, prior to the outbreak of war, was a captain in the United States Navy, and after secession, a captain in the Confederate navy. Historical Data Systems, comp., *U.S., Civil War Soldier Records and Profiles, 1861–1865*, American Civil War Research Database (hereinafter ACWRD). Also see Page, *Genealogy of the Page Family in Virginia*, 92.

think of the young ladies in those "diggins"?[6] I hope they are not all like those captured at Winchester. They seem to think that if the "Secesh women"[7] would come out and fight with them the war would soon end. There was a soldier here, who helped to guard them to Staunton,[8] and he says he never in his life heard such oaths as came from the lips of the Colonels' and Majors' wives.[9]

I assure you we envy those Yankee people the presence of our dear soldiers. Since you all left we have been as lonesome as "old cats." We seem to be in constant dread lest our army should fall back and leave us again in the hands of those miserable wretches. After you left we met with a great many of our friends, some of whom we had not dreamed of seeing, heard from a good many of our school mates through their Brothers and friends, who came up and introduced themselves, made many pleasant acquaintances and enjoyed ourselves generally. I think Genl Lee[10] is the sweetest old fellow I ever saw. I had quite a nice little chat with him that morning at Uncle Manns.[11] He told me that no soldier was to see his wife or sweet heart not until the war was over, so I concluded that he intended to end it before he came back from Pennsylvania. Mamma, Aunt Fannie and Harriot join me in much love to you.[12] All our street would send love if they knew of my writing. Please write soon and tell us all the news. Direct your next letter to Middleway Jefferson Co. If you direct to

---

6. A nineteenth-century colloquialism, meaning "vicinity."

7. Women who supported secession.

8. Staunton, Va.

9. These were Union women captured with their husbands at the Second Battle of Winchester in June 1863. At least eleven women were taken to Castle Thunder, a Confederate prison for civilians in Richmond. Although it appears they were soon released, this caused an uproar within the U.S. War Department, and Secretary of War Edwin M. Stanton mulled the possibility of arresting the wives of Confederate officers to ensure their safe return. Edwin M. Stanton to Colonel Ludlow, June 30, 1863, *War of the Rebellion: Official Records of the Union and Confederate Armies* (70 vols. in 128; Washington, 1880–1901) Ser. II, 6:62.

10. Major General Robert E. Lee, commander of the Army of Northern Virginia.

11. Mann P. Nelson, a physician and neighbor of the Scollay family, was married to Hannah E. Nelson and had two children, Elizabeth and Mann P., aged fifteen and thirteen, respectively. 1860 U.S. Census, Jefferson County, Va., population schedule, Middleway, p. 908, dwelling 417, family 401, Mann P. Nelson; digital image, *Ancestry.com* (http://ancestry.com : accessed April 24, 2017); citing NARA microfilm publication M653, roll 1355.

12. Harriot Scollay was Mollie's older sister. Frances B. "Fannie" Nelson was Mollie's aunt on the side of her mother, Sarah P. Nelson Scollay. All four lived together in 1860. See 1860 U.S. Census, Jefferson County, Va., population schedule, Middleway, p. 908, dwelling 416, family 400, Sarah P. Scollay; digital image, *Ancestry.com* (http://ancestry.com : accessed April 24, 2017); citing NARA microfilm publication M653, roll 1355.

Smithfield it may be miscarried and you know I should not like to lose
it.[13] Good bye. May a kind Providence shield you from all harm, and restore you in safety to your friends in "Dixie" is the sincere prayer of your
cousin Mollie S—

Westwood,[14] October 25th 1863

My own precious love

I got here safely this morning without an adventure of any kind; I did
not meet a living soul the whole way though I kept the main road all the
way. I have had about two hours sleep and feel quite fresh now. I made a
good walk of it last night, getting here at five minutes past 3 oclock. The
walk would have been a lovely one if I had not been so occupied with
thoughts of the dear one I had just left behind me, and anxious as I was
to get to my journeys end, I could not help wishing to linger near you.
I can't begin to describe to you, Mollie, what a gap your absence leaves;
I love you, to compare it with what *you* feel this morning for I *know*, beloved one, that you do indeed love me, even as I love you, and thus you
have by reference to your own heart, always at hand a far truer measure
of my emotions than you could get from any description I might give you.
But, my darling, it is a mighty great sorrow that I feel; the week I have
just passed with you, is so filled with tender memories, so full of love &
hope, that the present can but catch a tinge from it. And that picture I
have, how I did bless Aunt Fannie, this morning for letting me have it!
The sad look it has increases its value in my eyes, for a sad one was the
last expression I saw in your face. When I passed under your window last
night I was afraid to stop by but I might attract some ones attention to
you & I merely kissed my hand in passing. Did you see the act? I have
been uneasy ever since thinking you might not have noticed this slight
acknowledgement of your presence. I half expected you at that window,
darling, and I wanted so badly to stop & say one more good bye but, I
was afraid.

13. Mollie knew that there is a town named "Smithfield" in Virginia's Tidewater region
and anticipated the confusion that might occur if Wash used the local and historic name
of Smithfield to direct letters to a town known officially as Middleway.

14. Possibly a farm or plantation in Clarke County, Va., in the vicinity of Winchester,
where Wash was arrested. Thomas Daniel Gold refers to a "Westwood farm" in *History
of Clarke County, Virginia, and Its Connection with the War between the States* (Berryville, Va.:
Printed by C. R. Hughs, 1914), 115.

The Yankees have been here looking for horses—they rode through the field my mare was in and within fifty yards of her, but by some means or other did not see her. Am I not fortunate? Or rather I should say, is not providence kind? Cousin Hugh[15] has gone to Berryville to church[16] I shall not go until he returns, and I can learn from you whether there are any Yankees about. Fifteen Yankee deserters from Meade's army[17] passed here yesterday making for the Potomac. They report that Meade attacked Lee Saturday weak & was badly whipped.[18] Deserters can't be relied on, so I don't know whether to believe it or not. I can't undertake to write a regular letter now, with the means before me. When I tell you that in addition to what you see of the ink & paper, I am writing with a Turkey quill pen, you may know how I am laboring. As soon as I get to camp I will write you a good long letter. I am almost ashamed to send you this, but I would be glad to get a letter from you if it was nothing but piece of clothing paper with your name signed to it & telling me you were well and you see I judge you by myself. Love to *our* Mother & to all our Aunts and Cousins, and for yourself call on my heart for love at pleasure it is *all* your own. Good bye my precious darling. May God keep you and bless you, and restore us to each other soon.

As ever your truly devoted
Wash

Winchester Oct. 28th 1863

I am caught at last, my darling Mollie, and that too when I thought I was all safe & sound. Tom Randolph[19] & I were caught Monday while eating

15. Hugh Mortimer Nelson, II (1847–1915), lived in Clarke County, Va., and was the son of Hugh Mortimer Nelson (1811–62) and Anna Marie Adelaide Holker (1816–75). "Virginia Deaths, 1912–2014," database, *Ancestry.com* (http://ancestry.com : accessed April 24, 2017), entry for Hugh Mortimer Nelson, November 17, 1915, Clarke; citing "Virginia, Deaths, 1912–2014, Virginia Department of Health, Richmond, Virginia."

16. Berryville is located near Winchester in Clarke County, Va. Hugh probably attended Old Chapel, the Episcopal Church in Berryville.

17. George Gordon Meade, whom President Abraham Lincoln appointed to replace Joseph Hooker on June 28, 1863. McPherson, *Battle Cry of Freedom*, 652.

18. Wash must be referring to the Battle of Bristoe Station, October 14, 1863. The Union was actually successful.

19. Thomas H. B. Randolph (1843–1900) was the seventh of eight children of Robert C. Randolph, a physician and farmer, and Lucy M. Randolph. His brothers, William W. and Philip B. are mentioned in this collection. 1850 U.S. Census, Clarke County, Va., population schedule, 12th District, p. 200B, dwelling 462, family 462, Thomas H. Randolph;

our dinner, and not dreaming that there was a Yankee in twenty miles of us. We are very fortunate however. Have been treated as well as we could have been. We stayed at night with the officer of the Regiment & if it were not for this fact of guards being all around us you would not know we were prisoners. It is through the kindness of the commanding officer, Col Boyden[20] that I am now writing. Whither we will go from here I have no idea, nor in fact do I much care, if I am carried away from Dixie & from you, my own love, one place is as good as another. Probably I will pass thro' Smithfield to morrow. If so I will leave this for you—even if I should be allowed I think it better not to try to see you it would be an excuse for the soldiers to poke about the house, which would be anything but agreeable to you all. As soon as I was captured I was asked for letters or papers but fortunately had neither. And now, my precious one, don't grieve for me, I am as well off as a prisoner can be. Look forward to the time when we will meet again. I shall comfort myself with the idea that you are thus looking forward & not mourning my fate unnecessary. You may imagine what a comfort the time I spent with you will be to me. I have with me *all* your keepsakes. I have not time to write more. Love to all. If you have a chance, write to me & let me know what has become of you, will you dearest? And now, my beloved, good bye. We may not hear from each other for a long time but the fire of our love needs no more

---

digital image, *Ancestry.com* (http://ancestry.com : accessed April 24, 2017); citing NARA microfilm publication M432, roll 930. He was a student at the University of Virginia before the Civil War and enlisted in April 1861 as a corporal near his residence in Millwood, Clarke County, Va. He suffered a wound to the chest at the First Battle of Bull Run (June 1861) but returned to the army that December. He served as a member of General William Nelson Pendleton's staff. He was promoted to second lieutenant. He was captured at Rappahannock Station, Va., in December 1862. As a prisoner of war, he was confined at the Old Capitol Prison in Washington, D.C., and released in early 1863. As Wash notes in this letter, he was captured again in October 1863 and confined first at Camp Chase and then Johnson's Island. "Civil War Soldier Records and Profiles, 1861–65," database, *Ancestry.com* (http://ancestry.com : accessed on April 24, 2017), entry for Thomas Hugh Burwell Randolph. On June 12, 1865, he was released from prison after taking the Oath of Allegiance. On the subject of his imprisonment, see entry for Thomas H. B. Randolph, ACWRD.

20. Wash incorrectly identifies his captor as Boyden in both the letters and the memoir. He was perhaps captured by Colonel William H. Boyd (21st Pennsylvania Cavalry), who is listed as Wash's arresting officer in his service records. See Albert G. Brackett, *History of the United States Cavalry, from the Formation of the Federal Government to the 1st of June, 1863* (New York: Harper & Brothers, 1865), 329. Boyd was active in the vicinity of Middletown in the fall of 1863. Chester G. Hearn, *Six Years of Hell: Harpers Ferry during the Civil War* (Baton Rouge: Louisiana State University Press, 1996), 231.

fuel. *Our faith & trust cannot* fail. God almighty bless and keep you & restore us to each other soon. Earnestly prays, your ever devoted
   Wash

Middleway Dec 20th 1863

I found your letter here my dearest Wash on my return from Long Branch,[21] where Aunt F. and myself went to see little Hugh,[22] who had gotten his leg crushed in a wheat machine.[23] The limb was amputated below the knee. He stands the pain wonderfully, and bears his loss with Christian resignation. While in Clarke I saw a good deal of cousin Bettie Randolph.[24] She gave me all the details of your capture in which as you may imagine I was intensely interested. She read me a letter from her prisoner Brother, which was the first I had heard of you since your capture although I had made every possible effort to find out your whereabouts. The letter written from Camp Chase was never received. H. got a letter from your Ma in which she sent me word that she was gratified and thankful we had fancied each other. There was also a letter of sympathy from cousin Wm. P. He says Lieut. R.[25] and yourself are so well known for your good soldiery qualities that this little mishap will not injure your standing, and "sooner or later they will return to gladden the hearts of their friends, do good service to their country, and claim from their *sweet hearts* the reward of so much injury incurred in their behalf."

---

21. Long Branch Plantation is listed on the national register of historic places and is located in Millwood, Va. Hugh Mortimer Nelson purchased Long Branch Plantation from his uncle Phillip Nelson in about 1842. In 1860, the white members of the family consisted of Hugh M. Nelson Sr.; Adelaide Nelson (Hugh's wife); and two children, Nannie and Hugh Nelson Jr. In 1860, the plantation also had a population of twenty enslaved people. 1860 U.S. Census, Clarke County, Va., population schedule, p. 656 (stamped), dwelling 430, family 410, Hugh M. Nelson, NARA microfilm publication M653, roll 1341; 1860 U.S. Census, Clarke County, Va., slave schedules, p. 24, Hugh M. Nelson NARA microfilm publication M653, roll not identified.

22. Hugh Nelson Jr.

23. Probably a horse-powered reaper, or mechanical harvester, developed in the early 1830s and distributed fairly widely thereafter. After a steep decline in tobacco sales, upper-South states such as Virginia turned to wheat production. William L. Barney, *The Passage of the Republic: An Interdisciplinary History of Nineteenth Century America* (Lexington, Mass.: D.C. Heath, 1987), 24, 66.

24. Bettie B. Randolph (b. ca. 1831) lived in Clarke County, Va.

25. William Nelson Pendleton and Thomas Randolph, respectively.

How I would love to write more but I suppose my letters too are limited. Direct to care of L. P. W. Balch. Shepherdstown Va. All send love. Write again soon your loving and faithful friend M. N. S.

My kind regards and sympathy to Lieut Randolph. You must both keep cheerful hearts.

Middleway December 30th 1863

My dearest Wash

I have risen early this morning, so that I may not miss an opportunity of sending you another assurance of my love. Two whole months have passed since your capture, and only one single letter have I gotten in all that time. *Do* write as often as you can for I shall feel so anxious about you this Winter. In my last letter I did not have room to tell you of your Uncle Lucius Minor's death.[26] We did not hear any of the particulars, except that he died from the effects of his previous bad habits. He left cousin Fanny a double portion of his property. Cousin Jennie has gone back to H. H.[27] Gets 1,000 dollars a year, but intends staying only five months. I wrote to Aunt Jane[28] by Phil. He has gone *partially* engaged to Fannie. Don't some strange things happen in this world? Mamma and I send love. Aunt F. is still in Clarke. We heard from her last night. Is there a Lieut Newman[29] at Johnson's Island? Try and find him out. He is a nephew of

---

26. Lucius Horatio Minor (1810–63) was the fourth of six children of John Minor (1761–1816) and Lucy Landon Carter (1776–1855) of Fredericksburg, Va. He attended Yale College in the 1830s and is listed in the 1832 membership records of the secret literary society called the Brothers of Unity. "School Catalogs, 1765–1935," database, *Ancestry.com* (http://ancestry.com : accessed April 24, 2017), entry for Lucius Horatio Minor, 1880, Connecticut; citing "Educational Institutions, American Antiquarian Society, Worcester, Massachusetts."

27. Hickory Hill. See Mollie's letter to Wash dated June 22, 1864 (chap. 3).

28. Jane Crease Nelson, Wash's mother.

29. Possibly Anderson Moffett Newman Jr. (b. ca. 1840), a physician's son from Rockingham County, Va., who enlisted in Company I of the 1st Virginia Cavalry in May 1861. By February 1863, he had been promoted to second lieutenant. He was captured at Gettysburg, Pa., confined at Johnson's Island, Ohio, and exchanged on February 24, 1865. 1860 U.S. Census, Rockingham County, Va., population schedule, Harrisonburg, p. 452, dwelling 849, family 825, A. M. Newman, NARA microfilm publication M653, roll 1379; "Civil War Soldier Records and Profiles, 1861–1865," database, *Ancestry.com,* entry for Anderson Moffett Newman; citing The Virginia Regimental Histories Series. Also see entry for Anderson Moffett Newman, ACWRD.

our neighbor Mrs Hank,[30] and she is anxious to hear something about him. I should love to write a more satisfactory letter, but I have tried to say as much as possible in a small space. Heaven bless you, and soon restore you to me in safety is the constant prayer of your devoted.

    M

---

30. Serena Peale Hank, wife of William Hank (1796–1869), a traveling Methodist preacher. They lived in Frederick, Md., before moving to Middleway. See J. W. Hedges, ed., *Crowned Victors: The Memoirs of Over Four Hundred Methodist Preachers, Including the First Two Hundred and Fifty Who Died on This Continent* (Baltimore: Methodist Episcopal Book Depository, 1878), 509–11.

CHAPTER 2

Winter and Spring 1864

From One Prison to Another

This is the first of two chapters of correspondence from the tumultuous year of 1864. Wash was imprisoned at Johnson's Island and Mollie remained at her home in Middleway. As war raged on around them, the couple shared news and stories about their families and friends, as well as their private and intimate yearnings. In particular, both wished for an exchange of prisoners. Each move to a new prison brought Wash a brief glimmer of hope, only to be dashed by the prospect of prolonged imprisonment and separation from Mollie. Occasionally, Mollie wondered why Wash's connections could not help him get out of prison as a "special exchange" (an occasional negotiation on a man-to-man basis). Likewise, their experiences of writing and reading letters changed, as prison regulations forbade both Wash and Mollie from writing more than a single page. Letters also left and entered the prison unsealed so that a prison inspector could scan each letter for any military or political commentary or information.

"Home" Jan. 16 1864

My Dear Wash

I have set apart today for writing letters, and since *you* occupy the first place in my heart, my first letter shall be to you. After spending a week in the country, I have returned to settle down quietly in old Clip[1] for the rest of the Winter.

---

1. "Wizard Clip," or Middleway. See Middleway Historic District, Jefferson County, W.Va., Nomination to the National Register of Historic Places, 1973, on *West Virginia Di-*

That little visit did me a heap of good. I enjoyed it so much. We had three dinner parties given us, and had more cake and other nice things than I have seen since the War commenced. You must not think because I have been so gay, that I am less mindful of your unpleasant situation, for I assure you that there was not an hour in any day I did not think of you, and wish you could share my pleasure, and with what eagerness did I retire from the crowded room to devour the contents of your last two letters, which came to hand while I was there.

It was a great relief to me to hear that you had met with such kind friends. I wonder why yr cousin Josie has never written to you. Aunt Fannie returned from Clarke[2] a few days ago. She left Hugh sitting up. The danger all over.[3] Our relations in Hanover[4] were all well when we heard last. Did you ever get my letter telling of your Uncle Lucius Minor's death? The Lowry's[5] live in the two basement rooms at Edgewood, and manage for cousin Fannie.[6] I was requested the other day to get you to inquire if there is a Lieut. Clark[7] of Miss at Johnson's Island.

I am afraid you will think I keep you busy, but as I have asked the same favor of others of course I could not refuse to return it. We heard from Phil yesterday, above New Market.

I am almost afraid to write any more, for fear the letter may be thrown aside, and never reach you, as I had better stop.[8] Mama, Aunt Fannie, and H[9] send love to you. Harriet has written cousin Jennie[10] to let them

---

vision of Culture and History, http://www.wvculture.org/shpo/nr/pdf/jefferson/80004025 .pdf.

2. Clarke County, Va.

3. Here Mollie refers to the danger of gangrene setting in from the work accident and complications from the amputation mentioned in chap. 1.

4. Hanover County, Va., is located just over one hundred miles southeast of Clarke County.

5. Charles Y. and Frances E. Lowry, small farmers and neighbors living adjacent to the Minor's plantation, known as Edgewood. 1860 U.S. Census, Hanover County, Virginia, population Schedule, Upper Revenue District, p. 459, dwelling 290, family 287, Charles Y. Lowry, NARA microfilm publication M653, roll 1350.

6. Frances Berkley Minor, the second-born child of Catherine and Lucius Minor.

7. We have not been able to locate a Lieutenant Clark from Mississippi at Johnson's Island.

8. Mollie is worried about the one-page limit put on letters coming from and going into prisons.

9. Hugh Nelson Jr.

10. Jane Nelson was Wash's older sister and Mollie's cousin. She apparently went by "Jenny" or "Jennie" because that is how she signed the copy of Wash's prison memoir in 1866. George Washington Nelson memoir, 1866, Mss5:1N3360:1, Virginia Historical Society, Richmond, Va.

hear something about you. We all wrote by Phil. Do you ever see the paper's? I hear the prisoners have all been ordered to Point Lookout. I trust
the exchange will soon be resumed. Everard[11] is at Pt Lookout. Good bye.
Write again soon. Yrs devotedly

   M—

Saturday Night Jan. 30th 1864

My Dear Wash

I received your letter this evening and in compliance with your request, as well as the dictate of my own heart, I shall answer it immediately.

It is very strange you have never received any of my letters. I can't imagine what can be the reason unless they have been too long, and I hardly
think that can be, as you told me in your last, to write long letters, though
I have not yet ventured over three pages. You must not think unkindly
of me, or cease to write often, because you do not get my letters. I assure
you, I have written regularly ever since your capture and shall continue
to do so until you are released.

Your letters are such a comfort to me. You would be fully repaid for
the trouble (that is if it is a trouble) of writing them, if you could see
with what eagerness the contents are devoured. I feel very grateful to
Dr Minor and Mrs Massie[12] for their kindness to you. It reconciles me as
much more to your situation—now, that I can feel you are *at least* comfortable. You ask how I employ my time. I have done nothing lately but
read novels, and amongst them "Aurora Floyd" and "No Name", which I
think you had just read when you were here.[13] As to your being a lawyer.

---

11. Everard Meade (1843–1913) was a student in Clarke County, Va., when he joined
the 4th Virginia Infantry on June 2, 1861, at age 18. In 1862, Meade was wounded at the
Second Battle of Bull Run (August), and at the Battle of Antietam (September). He fell
into Union hands on October 9, 1863 and eventually sent to Point Lookout, Md. He was paroled at Point Lookout. He was exchanged on April 27, 1864. "Compiled Service Records
of Confederate Soldiers Who Served in Organizations from the State of Virginia," digital
images, *Fold3* (http://www.fold3.com : accessed April 24, 2017); Everard Meade (Fourth
Infantry, Virginia); citing NARA microfilm publication M324, roll not identified.

12. Possibly Elizabeth F. Massie, wife of the farmer Nathaniel Massie (b. 1795) and
mother of D. Rhodes Massie (b. 1836). 1860 U.S. Census, Augusta County, Va., population
schedule, North Subdivision, p. 1096, dwelling 1940, family 1945, Elizabeth F. Massie,
NARA microfilm publication M653, roll 1333.

13. Mary Elizabeth Braddon, *Aurora Floyd: A Novel* (Richmond: West & Johnston, 1863)
and Wilkie Collins, *No Name* (London: Sampson Low, Son & Co., 1862). Collins's novel
followed his very successful *The Woman in White* (London: Sampson Low, Son & Co., 1860).

I never was very partial to that profession, but if you think you can succeed—as such—I am perfectly willing. All send love. Good night. Your true and loving

Mollie.

I suppose you never got my letter telling you of Fannie's engagement to Phil. He left us some time ago, and we heard he had gotten out safely.

Johnson's Island Feb 9th 1864

I wrote you yesterday, my darling Mollie, what I thought would be my last letter from this place, but your's of Jan 30th has just been handed me, & I can't resist the desire to answer it at once. To think unkindly of you, or to cease writing to you, are both impossibilities for me: how *could* I do either, my darling, when I love you & *you only* with my whole heart? So far from being a trouble to me, writing to you has always been my dearest pleasure, and you can imagine how I must value this privilege under my personal circumstances—remember too, I never complained of your not writing, but of my bad fortune in not getting your letters; the fickle Goddess has already changed her mood & is beginning to smile upon me—see how soon I got your last letter, written only nine days ago. It is mighty sweet in you to tell me what a comfort my letters are to you; I can easily imagine so, if I may compare them with what yours are to me. They can't give you much satisfaction though, they are so short & cramped: there is no limit or measure for the feeling that goes from my heart to you, & how can it express itself in the narrow limit of a page? But I don't mean to complain. I am very thankful that this much is granted me. I have room enough to tell you how entirely I *do* love you; and that my faith & trust in you grows brighter every day—and with these land marks, your own heart, my own love, will supply all that I would say, and will speak for me far more eloquently than any words I could use. To day is Ash Wednesday, and we have had the services of our church[14] in this room. The Rev. McHelen[15] (a fellow prisoner) holds services two or three

14. Prison religious meeting likely conducted in the particular services of the Episcopal Church, with "our church" implying the shared Episcopal faith of Mollie and Wash.

15. No prisoner by that last name has been found. Religious ceremonies in prisons were quite common. See Michael P. Gray, *The Business of Captivity: Elmira and Its Civil War Prison* (Kent: Kent State University Press, 2001), 111–13; Roger Pickenpaugh, *Captives in Gray: The Civil War Prisons of the Union* (Tuscaloosa: University of Alabama Press, 2009), 110–12.

times a week. You would be surprised at the interest manifested in them. This imprisonment will, with God's blessing, prove eternal salvation to many of us: Truly, *"He* doeth all things well."[16]

What do you mean by succeeding as a lawyer? Do you mean, making a fortune, or doing my duty & benefiting my fellows? Maybe you mean both. With *you* for my blessing & comfort, I feel sure of success in most anything. However there is very little probability that the Law will get me; unless perhaps it comes upon me in the shape of the hangman's noose; and I fancy neither you nor I would relish my performing under those circumstances. You didn't tell me what you thought of "Aurora Floyd" and "No Name." Love to all. Continue to write to me *here.* Good by, dearest, God bless you Always your devoted Wash Nelson.

"Home" Feb. 26th 1864

I have not written to you before my dear Wash, because I saw by the papers that some of the prisoners had been removed from Johnson's Island, and not knowing that you might be among the number, I thought I would wait before writing to hear from you again. Yours of the 9th was handed me last night, so I eagerly embrace the first opportunity of sending a reply. You mention having written the day before that letter to cousin Jennie in answer to one received from her a day or two ago. Hers was dated the 6th of this month, and up to that time they had not heard a word from you. Aunt Jane[17] says she is sick for the sight of a line from you, and begs me to ask you to write her. If you will write me a nice little *friendly* letter, I will allow her the privilege of reading it. I could not possibly let any other eyes than my own read the others, that is, after they come into my possession for I expect those sacred pages are scanned by many a desecrating eye before they ever reach me. I can not tell you anything of cousin Randolph, as we never hear anything of them now. Cope was quite sick after you left, and it was feared for some time that he was in a decline, but I believe he has entirely recovered. So I heard in Clarke. Please remember me to Lt. Randolph. I am so glad to hear of the

---

16. Mark 7:37. Wash slightly misquotes the King James Bible, which reads "He hath done all things well."

17. Wash's mother, Jane Crease Nelson.

religious feeling among the prisoners. All send much love to you. Write
soon. Yrs as ever
      Mollie

Johnson's Island Feb. 26th 1864

My darling Mollie
      To day has been so mild & pleasant, that, considering this alone, I could
almost fancy myself in dear "old Virginia." And I cannot let the night go
by without writing to tell you that to day you have been, if possible, more
than ever in my thoughts. Will you think me foolish when I tell you my
chief employment has been making different combinations of the letters
in your name? I even invoked my muse, and turned these combinations
into verse—or, more correctly rhyme. I would give you a specimen but
for the fact that my space is so limited. I think I see a smile upon your lips
even now, a sweet, kind smile though, because your heart tells you it is
the foolishness of love. Let me tell you that I did not feel in the least bit
foolish during my occupation far from it. Wrapt in my theme[18] I culled
the sweet & unfaded flowers that memory "grew" around me, and passing by unchilled the blank of the present, my spirit felt the fruition of its
constant hope. I was no longer alone, a loved companion joined her fate
to mine, fair breezes, gentle & refreshing showers our pos[i]tion. Yes I
was happy, sublimely happy. Surely they are to be pitied who cry down
the culture of the ideal, or as they please to term it, "building air castles."
Either they have never loved, or else they are of the member of those who
attest the truth of the lines "Ah! It is the worst of pain, to love & not be
loved again."[19] I thank God for the power, with which he has endowed the
soul, of abstracting itself from its surroundings, and finding sweet solace
in a sphere of dreams and visions and returning, refresh & invigorate
its companion the body. Without this play of the imagination, memory
would be a curse for it would be sweetened by no hope in the future,
and we might well say "That a sorrow's crown of sorrow is remembering
happier things."[20] I am writing, my darling, just as I feel because I want

---

18. Writing poetry.
      19. Anacreon, "Gold," in *Specimens of the Poets and Poetry of Greece and Rome*, ed. William
Peter (Philadelphia: Carey and Hart, 1847), 50.
      20. Lord Alfred Tennyson, "Locksley Hall," in *Poems* (London: Edward Moxon, 1842),
2: 92–111.

you to know that my love, supported by the assurance of yours, makes me happy, & that I wait patiently for the realization of my hopes. I have no fear in showing you how completely I am in your power, for, "perfect love casteth out fear"[21] & besides, I am certain of the truthfulness of your nature. In case you shouldn't get my last letter, I will mention again, that I received yours of the 5th & answered it a day or two ago. And let me beg you again, not to talk of giving up writing, because your letters don't reach me regularly. Never to hear from you at all, would be too much for me. Love to *our* mother, & to all. How are matters between Fannie & Phil? "In status quo," or settled? Good bye, dearest. God bless you. Your loving & devoted

Wash Nelson

"Home," March 2nd 1864

My dear Wash

I had just been wishing for a letter when yours of the 23rd was handed me.

I have been very fortunate lately, receiving on an average, one, and sometimes, two letters a week. Hope you will continue to write often, and I shall do likewise, now that I know there is a possibility of my letters reaching their destination. It would not take me long to guess the meaning of the valentine you mentioned, but the sender has mistaken the church. I don't think we would go quite as far as the "Old Fork," while there is a certain little church by the name of "Grace," so much nearer home. A few nights ago, I stepped over to Mr Hanks to sit until bed time, and staid rather later than usual. No one at home knew where I was, and among numerous conjectures, it was finally concluded, that your humble servant had started to walk to "Johnson's Island." I should love dearly to see a certain prisoner there, but don't think I could walk *quite that far*, were I sure of not *freezing* before reaching my journey's end.

Wash, have you ever heard any thing of Fenny Wrenn?[22] His friends have never heard of him since the battle of "Gettysburg." Don't know

---

21. John 4:18.

22. Fenton Eley Wrenn (1839–63) was born in Wight County, Va., and attended Hanover Academy and the University of Virginia. He left school and enlisted as a private in the 3rd Virginia Infantry on July 8, 1861, and was promoted to sergeant and second lieutenant in 1862. At the Battle of Antietam, Wrenn was wounded by shrapnel in the chest. He re-

whether he was killed or is a prisoner. Our boys *at school* are well, and doing well, plenty to *eat* and *wear*. They expect to have vacation about the first of April, when we hope to see them.[23] I wish you could be exchanged before that time. Ma is quite poorly, and has been for some time. I have been very much interested lately in *"Say and Seal."*[24] Didn't like "Aurora Floyd" much. "No Name" a little better. All send love.

    Yrs devotedly

    M—

Johnson's Island March 8 1864

I send you, my dear Mollie, a ring made here in prison. I had it made expressly for you. I fear it is too large. Wear it for my sake, darling. I had hoped long ago to have put upon your finger with my own hands the pure circle of gold which should emblem the purity & constancy of my love; this pleasure has been denied me, and until this privilege is mine, I know you will wear & prize the little token of love I send. Oh if I could only accompany it. I received a nice long letter from Mrs Massie to day; she asked very particularly after you. Says she wants our photographs & wants them taken together. Wouldn't I give my right arm for the power to oblige her! She speaks of you as the "glorious fact." Alluding to my reply to her question in a former letter as to whether you were pretty, she adding "of course *you* think so & will say so." And I replied, "there is no think so or say so about it, it is a glorious fact." And now she always speaks of you as the *"glorious fact."* I don't mind telling you these little things, you know I am no flatterer, & I am not afraid of the truth spoiling you. You have not mentioned Fanny & Phil lately—how is their affair progressing? I suppose Phil changed his tactics before the desired end was accomplished. I have written a very small page this time, to ensure its

---

joined his regiment in October 1862, and served until being killed in Pickett's Charge at Gettysburg (ACWRD). John Lipscomb Johnson, *The University Memorial: Biographical Sketches of Alumni Who Fell in the Confederate War* (Baltimore: Turnbull Brothers, 1871), 842–45. See also Drew Gilpin Faust, *This Republic of Suffering: Death and the American Civil War* (New York: Vintage, 2008), 128.

23. Mollie has written the preceding sentences in code. "Boys" means soldiers, "school" means army, and "vacation" probably means the start of the spring campaign. Mollie hopes to see them because they are in occupied country, and she wishes that Wash is exchanged by then, so that he can rejoin the Confederate army.

24. Susan Warner and Anna Bartlett Warner, *Say and Seal* (Philadelphia: J. B. Lippincott & Co., 1860).

going through. Love to all. That God may bless & keep you, my darling, is the earnest prayer of your loving & devoted

Wash Nelson

Johnson's Island March 14 1864

Your letter, my darling, has just been handed me—it was written to day one week ago. If as you were fearful of doing, I am violating the Sabbath. I do it ignorantly, for I am unconscious of sinning against God by my present act—far from it—I always feel nearer to Him, when thinking of & writing to you; my heart is constantly thanking him for the precious blessing he has given me in your love. And oh! how sweet & peaceful the picture, that now arises before me, of us two living together in the fear & love of God, upholding each other in the Christian race[25] his faithful servants during this life, & then together praising him through an endless eternity. Mollie dearest one, my love for you is so absorbing, that I can look upon nothing as happiness unless shared by you; and all I need to decide that any condition of life will be a happy one, is to know that you will be with me. Need I tell you how sweet the assurance is that your thoughts are often with me in my Island prison? And to be told too that I am the one dear to your heart—my love drinks in with eager joy the assurances of its full return. Your letter, written last Sunday, was a good work, for it has gladdened one of the lousy pilgrims of earth. You ask me how I spend my Sundays—Our minister is in "Dixie" by this time—he left us about two weeks ago; but we still have the beautiful service of our church. I read it for our room.[26] The rest of the day I spend in reading some good books, of which, thanks to Mrs. Massie, I have a good many, and in talking—late in the evening I lie down on my "bunk," and think your own heart will tell you of whom—then too at night we have a grand singing of hymns. Do you remember my reading the service at your house once? If you have forgotten it doubtless I can recall it to your mind by the simple word "Tychicus"[27] & if that doesn't suffice, I will add

---

25. See Hebrews 12:1. "Therefore, since we are surrounded by so great a cloud of witnesses, let us also lay aside every weight and sin that clings so closely, and let us run with perseverance the race that is set before us."

26. Wash implies reading from the *Book of Common Prayer*.

27. A minor figure in early Christianity and friend of Paul. It is most likely that the Book of Common Prayer's lectionary readings for the service that Wash recalls in this letter included one of the five readings in which Tychicus is named (Acts 20: 4; Ephesians 6:21;

"Kinloch[28] & laughter["]. You mention Miss Lilly D.[29] I am much obliged for her sympathy—is Maj. Dearing[30] still persevering in that quarter? I am mighty sorry to hear that your mother continues unwell. I trust your uneasiness will prove groundless—in any event, my darling, we are all in God's hands. You have learned to look upon him as a loving Father, who will give you "help in every time of need." That He may comfort you & bless you is the earnest prayer of your

    own devoted Wash Nelson
  — love to all —

The following statements are written in pencil on the reverse of the letter, probably by Mollie.

I can get no new letter, so I read the old one.

    O! it is so cruel in the Yankee's not to permit an exchange of prisoners.

Sept 6th 1864

Leiut Scott. Hateful Yankee was captured today. I am so delighted. I hope the dear Rebs will pay him for his impudence. I reckon he is done *lording* it over Clip for a while at least.

Johnson's Island March 23rd 1864

My darling Mollie

    Your letter of the 14th was received this morning. I am glad you are so hopeful on the exchange question—for my own part I am afraid to give too great wings to my hopes on this subject: disappointment would be so much harder to bear. We have been exchanged so often, & so often disappointed that it is no wonder I am sceptical. I take everything "cum

---

Colossians 4:7; 2 Timothy 4:1; Titus 3:12). Perhaps the pronunciation of his name titillated those in attendance.

28. Possibly a reference to their cousin, Kinloch Nelson of Hanover County, Va. See Mollie's letter to Wash, May 21, 1865 (chap. 5).

29. Lily Dandridge was a well-known debutante of Winchester, Va. See Margaretta Barton Colt, *Defend the Valley: A Shenandoah Family in the Civil War* (Oxford, England: Oxford University Press, 1994), 381.

30. While the military rank is incorrect, later letters suggest that this is likely a reference to James Griffin Dearing (1840–65) of Lynchburg, Va., who enlisted in April 1861 as captain of Company D, 38th Battalion Heavy Artillery. "Civil War Soldier Records and Profiles, 1861–1865," database, *Ancestry.com* (http://ancestry.com : accessed April 24, 2017), entry for James Griffin Dearing; citing "The Virginia Regimental Histories Series."

grano salis" [with a grain of salt]—hope for the best, but still don't let my peace of mind depend upon it. A Lt. Col. in the "bunk" next to mine, has just remarked, "When I *am* exchanged I will feel as I imagine one does who has just gotten religion; I know I shall be in a state between crying & laughter, and shaking hands with everybody."

You speak of the pleasure my mother & sister will have in seeing me, and then conclude that they will have that pleasure before you. Do you know, my vanity, not that either, but my love is pleased with the thought that you grudge them this *first* sight? You are mistaken though in supposing I won't venture in your direction again very soon. *You* are in all my thoughts—the source & centre of all my hopes—how could I keep away from you? Even my liberty seems tame & cheerless, until your presence brightens & gladdens the picture. I told you once I would not be so extravagant as to say "I loved you as man never loved before"—but indeed I feel that way now. Be sure of one thing dearest, that as soon after I am free as *duty* will permit, I will be with *you*. It is very hard to realize now, that there ever was a time when all a body had to do to see his lady-love, was simply to take the first train, and away he'd go to his journey's end without anyone to interfere with or stop him. Well maybe we would not have appreciated each other as fully under such favorable circumstances. I read an essay last night in our "club,"[31] entitled "The Lover's Ideal." It was very much applauded—it ought to have been good, for my ideal was a reality, and the inspiration of a great love was upon me. Thank Fannie for letting you tell me all you know. You didn't tell me much, but enough for me to set Phil down as the most fortunate & the happiest man, next to myself, of my acquaintance. I hope *our* mother has recovered as you didn't mention her. Love to all. God bless you, my precious Love. Yours in the sweetest bonds,

Wash Nelson

Johnson's Island March 27th 1864

It is Sunday evening, my own love; and such a lovely evening too—nearly every one around me is asleep and the room is perfectly quiet. I have been lying down for the last hour or so, but my thoughts have been so busy I could not sleep. I have been thinking of you more intensely than

---

31. The prison literary society, which Wash attended regularly.

ever. So, thinking you won't object, I have determined to give you a page of my thoughts; and they are all mighty happy thoughts, for they are bright, sweet hopes—hopes that I feel are nearer their fruition. My belief that we will soon leave for "Dixie" has been growing every day. You, dearest, can imagine how much happiness such a belief must bring me, for does not my heart feel that it will soon again drink in the sweet smiles of its peerless queen? And then, something tells me that she who loves me & is so true, will not make it long before she crowns my wishes. Tell me, darling, is it not a prophetic voice that whispers this?

All my happiness is in your hands, and there I leave it without a doubt or a fear. There never was a greater libel against true love than those lines of Miss Landon's—

> "Tis not kindness keeps a lover
> He must feel the chain he wears,
> All the sweet enchantment's over,
> When he has no anxious cares."[32]

Faith & trust *must* enter largely into *true* love, and they admit no such thing as "anxious cares." I don't look upon love as simply a "sweet enchantment," that implies it may be broken, but rather as a soul-filling joy, resting upon & nurtured by the blessed peace of perfect confidence. Such at least, dearest, is the nature of my love for you. And such, I know, is the only love you would value. I stopped writing a few moments to watch a "Baptizing" in Lake Erie. That ceremony has just been performed upon 12 prisoners. It made me feel very solemn, as I watched the poor fellows march out into the Lake, loose ice floating on it, singing their hymns— and the guard drawn up on the shore. The *ladies* of the Island also graced the occasion with their presence. Tried my best to distinguish the kind of dress & the style of the bonnets they wore, but you know, I am not "au fait" [up-to-date] in such matters; so my ideas are not in sufficient shape to be expressed.[33] My page is filled. Good bye. God grant I may be with you soon. Love to all.

As ever your devoted Wash Nelson

---

32. "Cottage Courtship," *The Complete Works of L. [Letitia] E. [Elizabeth] Landon* (Boston: Crosby, Nichols, Lee, 1860), 289.

33. Here Wash describes a common civilian excursion on the lake. Gray, "Captivating Captives," 16–32. Pickenpaugh, *Captives in Gray*, 100.

The following letter far exceeds the one-page limit enforced by prison censors. Mollie's presumption that Wash has been released must account for the different tone and inclusion of so much detail in this letter. In fact, this letter likely never reached Wash in prison. Mollie addressed the envelope to General Pendleton's Headquarters, where she presumed Wash was going after the exchange. An "R" written in pencil indicates that the letter was returned.

"Home" April 5th 1864

My dear Wash

I heard through cousin Bettie Randolph that you were expected by the "Flag of truce boat," which was due last Thursday week, so I suppose by this time, you are enjoying the sweets of freedom, in our dearly loved Confederacy. Would that I could have been in Dixie, to welcome you home! but alas! that privilege was denied me, and I fear it will be a long *long* time before we meet, for I must forbid your coming to the valley again, until you can come with safety, and I believe it is the general impression that our army will not be here this Summer. O! I trust we are not destined to be shut up in the Yankee lines all Summer. We are surrounded by them on all sides now. No one can get out of town—even to get a stick of wood, and what we are to do I don't know, but I trust the Lord will provide. We had an old house in the yard pulled down to burn, and I hope by the time that is gone, the Yankees will be removed. I have not been able to get my letters from Shepherdstown since they came, so I have not heard from you for some time. Before, I used to hear quite often. The last letter received was the one, containing the ring. Did you write afterwards?[34] I was restricted to such short letters, that I could not derive much pleasure from writing them, and now, I have got so much to tell, I hardly know where to begin. In one of your letters you asked me what I thought when I heard of your capture, but don't think I ever answered the question.

Really I was so much surprised that I scarcely had time for thought. At first we heard that it was Lieut's. Phil Nelson and J. Randolph, but I knew directly there had been some mistake made in the name, so I gave up all

---

34. Here Mollie refers to the letter Wash wrote to her on March 8, 1864. She had not received the letters posted since that time, even though they are included in this collection.

hope of seeing or hearing from you until after the War. Notwithstanding, I made every possible effort to find out your whereabouts, and I don't think after I heard of your capture that I ever gave way to my feelings but once, and that was, when I found that all my efforts had proved in vain.

However, *of course*, the reports were put out that "Miss Mollie was terribly distressed, grieving herself to death" &c, and every one imagines I am very thin, so you may expect to find me a mere skeleton when you come. By the way, Wash, I do not think our Westwood friends are very good hands to keep a secret, for when I was staying in the country, I was told that our engagement was the general topic of conversation in the neighborhood, and in a roomful, one day—cousin Lizzie[35] remarked to me, that the daguerreotype Wash had, was very much like me. I could not help feeling amused at her. She had an old piece of a comb, you had left there, which she was very anxious I should have, but I told her she might have it, to keep for your sake. They have been *very* kind however, and I hope I am not ungrateful.

It was my painful task to communicate a few days ago to a friend of mine, the sad intelligence, of her lover's death.

Poor child! she is completely heart-broken, and I feel most tenderly for her. On her 18th birthday, they were to have been married, death alone preventing; and as it has pleased God to take him, she says, she cannot help praying that they may be united in Heaven on that day. This cruel war has crushed so many-many young hearts, and I fear the same trial is in store for many more. O! may Heaven avert this blow from me. Since I have seen Mollie's distress, it has made me cling to you more than ever.

You will not be wearied by this part of my letter, as I know you will feel interested in anybody that I love. It is said that the darkest hour is just before day. For the last few weeks every thing has looked very gloomy to us, so I trust our day of deliverance is not far off. A negro reg[imen]t went up from Charlestown to Winchester and camped last night at Bunker Hill.

They carried every thing before them. I trust they will not get here. I have the greatest horror of them. The Yankee's have enroled in this country black as well as white. The enroling officer came here, but we told him that all of our negro men had gone to the Yankee's except one, and he was afflicted, so he did not take his name. It was galling to the flesh I assure you, but this is only one of the numerous indignations, to

---

35. Elizabeth Nelson (1845–80) was the eighth child of Mann Page Nelson (1800–1888) and the sixth child he had with his second wife, Lydia Ann Kounslar (1815–52).

which we are every day subjected; however we bear it all cheerfully as it
is for the good of our Confederacy. Harriet and I spent to day at Aunt
Betsey's, though it was snowing hard, and we had to wade through water
to get there.

We have to stay together as much as possible, in order to keep up our
spirits. There has been a great deal of disagreeable, wet weather lately,
which, I think, is calculated to make one feel sad.

Fannie has heard from Phil only once since he left. It is strange he
does not write, but perhaps his silence is owing to the difficulty of getting letters in now. Before he left here, he went to the country and spent
several weeks, and it was then they became engaged, after which he came
back here to see her. Fannie came down and staid until he left. They
occupied *our* little room. Those old walls if they could talk could tell
some *grand old tales*. I have often pictured to myself the meeting between
cousin Jennie and your self. I know they were both delighted to see you.
You must write me a long letter to make up for lost time, and tell me
all about your imprisonment. I know that you were treated a great deal
worse than you would allow, but now that you are free, I want to know all
about it. Don't forget to have your daguerreotypes taken for me. I would
rather have the whole figure, standing, if you can get a good likeness in
that way, but if not any other will do. Direct your letter to Middleway, Jeff.
Co. Care of Col. Nadenboush,[36] Staunton. He has command there and
will be likely to know of all the opportunities down this way. Give my love
to Aunt Jane and coz Jennie. Tell the latter to answer my letter. All send
much love to you. Please tell me of cousin Jeff Page when you write. May
heaven bless you and soon restore us to each other prays your loving and
    faithful
    Mollie

---

36. John Quincy Adams Nadenbousch (1824–92) was from Berkeley County, Va. (now
W.Va.). He was a prominent local figure, holding positions such as mayor of Martinsburg,
Va., and belonging to the influential Independent Order of Odd Fellows. His family papers
are held at the Virginia Historical Society.

CHAPTER 3

May–December 1864

"There Is Always Some Jonah"

As Mollie's letter dated April 5, 1864, indicated, the lovers expected to be reunited in that year. Yet one thing prevented this reunion: the slipshod exchange efforts being pursued by the Union and the Confederacy. Wash was frequently on the move in the spring and summer of 1864. In May 1864, Wash was a patient in Hammond General Hospital at Point Lookout Prison. Having recovered from his illness, he returned to the prison at Point Lookout the next month and was assigned to the officer's camp. While Johnson's Island was designated to confine only Confederate officers, Point Lookout held both officers and enlisted men. Prisoners there were segregated by rank, which helped break down command structures and prevent organized resistance. In practice, it also meant that Union and Confederate officers typically received better treatment than the enlisted men. Wash remained at Point Lookout until the end of June, when he moved to Fort Delaware. By the end of October, Wash had been moved to Fort Pulaski, located near Savannah, Georgia.

Hammond General Hospital Point Lookout
May 23 1864

Your letter of the 8th,[1] my darling, just received, has brought me untold comfort. Since I know I can still hear from my beloved, I am myself again, happy & almost well. I am very much better, only a little weak now, two or three more letters from you will make me as well as ever. I am nicely fixed here—a small room, all to myself, where I can read, write,

---

1. The letter to which Wash refers is not included in the collection at Virginia Tech.

think or sleep, just when I please. When I am lonesome, I go into some
one of the rooms around me, and talk as much as I please. The rest &
quiet here are a great relief, after the crowd at "Johnson's Island" that
you could never for one moment get away from. And you thought me exchanged? I had concluded you were laboring under some such mistake.
How I wish I had that long letter you speak of,[2] though if wishing would
do any good, I'd wish a great deal more than that. Do you remember that
prayer in which we are taught to pray for "minds always contented with
our present condition"?[3] I have need to repeat that prayer mighty often.
And I fear with mighty poor results. By the way, don't write such short
letters; I received four pages from Mrs. Massie this morning. She speaks
of you, as indeed she does in all her letters, rightly considering *that* the
most pleasing subject to me. All you tell me about Cousin Wm & Ranny[4]
is news. I have not heard a word from any of them except through you.
I wonder Randolph don't have his wife with him; I thought that was his
object in getting his present place. One of these days, with somebody's
permission, I will set such mistaken creatures, as Ranny a good example.
I am so glad dearest, you didn't know I was sick—to know that you were
unhappy would not have helped me the most in the world. Don't be uneasy about me any longer. You shall hear from me often—if my letters
go straight. How does "Clip" look this spring? Has your mother entirely
recovered? My best love to her & to all. How I wish I could write you as
long a letter as I would like. Could I show you my whole heart, you would
see how supreme is your rule, how tenderly & devotedly I love. God Bless
you, my darling

    Your devoted—Wash

These lines appear on the back of the letter: "Long letters not delivered. Examiner[.]" *Thus, a prison censor, or "examiner," read Wash's above request for
longer letters and warned Mollie not to write one. Once Mollie received the letter,
she angrily wrote a response for posterity:* "You hateful dog! What business had

    2. Wash must be referring to Mollie's letter to Wash at Johnson's Island, April 5, 1864.

    3. "Forms of Prayer to be used in Families: Morning Prayer," *Book of Common Prayer, and
Administration of the Sacraments, and Other Rites and Ceremonies of the Church, According to the Use
of the Protestant Episcopal Church in the United States of America* (Philadelphia: J. B. Lippincott
& Co., 1865), 363.

    4. William Nelson Page Jr. (1840–61) and Isham Randolph Page (1834–1923), two
of seven children of William Nelson Page (b. 1803), of Cumberland County, Va. See 1850
U.S. Census, Cumberland County, Va., population schedule, p. 292B, dwelling 149, family
149, William W. Page [erroneous spelling of William N. Page], NARA microfilm publication
M432, roll 941.

you writing on my letter." *In her next letter to Wash, dated June 6, 1864, she notifies him of the examiner's message.*

Hammond General Hospital Point Lookout May 30th 1864

I was glad to learn from your last letter, my darling Mollie, that some of the many letters I have written had reached you. You may relieve your mind altogether, as regards to my health, I am well, and expect to leave the Hospital for camp to day or tomorrow. You are wrong though in your prejudice against hospitals. This is certainly the best berth I have had since my capture, and I regret the change. I remember Miss Lizzie Selden[5] mighty well; and I remember almost as well a nice collation of cold Turkey, pies, cakes &c, which she provided, and of which I partook most fully the first & only time I ever saw her. And she is married. I congratulate Capt. Dimmock on his good fortune.[6] I have never been able to find out whether Everard[7] is here or not; if I do come across him I will let you know. Ask Fanny please to give you a positive answer for my sake— tell her to remember how I took her into my confidence "made her my book, wherein my soul recorded" "The history of all its secret thoughts."[8]

When you see your sister Annie[9] again, give her my very best love; I often think of the evening you & I spent with her—I wonder whether we will get lost, the next ride we take through those woods? That was the most miserable time I ever spent not because we were lost though, that was a relief if anything—you remember that line of Tennyson's "A sorrow's crown of sorrow, is remembering happy days"[10] I suppose it is one of the same principles of contrast, that we love, when in happy circum-

---

5. Elizabeth Selden Dimmock (1842–1930). "Virginia Deaths, 1912–2014," database, *Ancestry.com*, entry for Elizabeth Lewis Dimmock [Elizabeth Lewis Selden], October 20, 1930, Gloucester, Va.; citing "Virginia, Deaths, 1912–2014, Virginia Department of Health, Richmond, Virginia."

6. Charles H. Dimmock married Elizabeth L. Selden October 14, 1863, in Richmond, Va.

7. Everard Meade.

8. Both quotations are from Shakespeare's *Richard III*, act 3, scene 5.

9. Anne Lloyd Scollay (1825–68) was the second-born child of Samuel Scollay and his first wife, Harriot Lowndes. Technically, she was Mollie's half-sister.

10. Lord Alfred Tennyson, "Locksley Hall," in *Poems* (London: Edward Moxon, 1842), 2: 99. Wash most likely quoted Tennyson from memory, as the published text reads, "That a sorrow's crown of sorrow is remembering happy things."

stances, to look back at some "dies irae" [day of wrath], which we thought we should never get over.

You have not quite relieved me from my difficulty about Mrs Dangerfield yet. If I should write to her, it would never do to direct my letter to Mrs. Dangerfield.[11] Can you help me there? Either her own name, or her husbands will do. If you begin to think me troublesome, with my questions, I will quote scripture to you—"Bear ye one another's burdens,"[12] which means help each other out of difficulties.

I wonder what sort of a description you would give me of yourself. Not one that I would begin to accept I reckon. My memory is very faithful on this point, and would not quiet suffer to do injustice to yourself. Love to all. Good bye, my darling.

Believe me, as ever, your devoted
Wash[13]

June 3rd 1864

Why is it my dear Wash that you have not been exchanged? Until last night, I had not heard for so long that I was sure you were with your friends in "Dixie," but alas! Your letter of the 29th assures me of the *sad, sad, sad* fact that you are still a prisoner. I am afraid you have been sick again. Tell me. Since I last wrote, I have been quite sick myself, but am entirely well now, and feel better than I have done for many months. Am still thin, but improving in flesh. Tell me about Lt. R.[14] when you write again, so that I may let his friends know. They have not heard from him since early in March. I sent him a letter from his Mother, talking of his Brother Willie's death. He was killed in the last terrible battle.[15] Harriot

---

11. Rebecca H. and John B. Dangerfield of Alexandria, Va. 1860 U.S. Census, Alexandria County, Va., population schedule, Alexandria, p. 847, dwelling 1158, family 1266, J. B. Dangerfield, NARA microfilm publication M653, roll 1331.

12. Galatians 6:2.

13. Penned in an unrecognizable hand, beneath Wash's signature, is the sentence, "Mollie says you want to know something about my ladyship."

14. Lieutenant Thomas H. B. Randolph.

15. William "Willie" Welford Randolph of Clarke County enlisted as a private in the 2nd Virginia Infantry in 1861 at the age of twenty-four. He was promoted to captain in April 1862 and lieutenant colonel in April 1864. He died on May 5, 1864, from wounds received at the Battle of the Wilderness. "Compiled Service Records of Confederate Soldiers Who Served in Organizations from the State of Virginia," digital images, *Fold3* (http://www.fold3 .com : accessed April 24, 2017); William W. Randolph (Private, 2nd Virginia Infantry); citing NARA microfilm publication M324, roll 0378.

heard from Robert P. He had seen cousin Jennie lately. All were well. Phill safe up to the 15th.[16] Cousin Hugh has gone for cousin Julia, and we are anxiously looking forward to his return. There is a note here for you from coz. Jennie, written some time ago. I don't know about sending it with mine for fear it may be too much, and you would not receive either. Do you still correspond with Mrs. Massie? Give my love to her when you write. Ma, Aunt F., and H. send love. Do write again soon. Don't you expect to be exchanged? My letters go through so many hands even to get to the office, and of course are read by almost every one.[17] You must not think them *cold*. I scarcely know how to write them.

Yrs. M—

June 6 1864

The girls have all gone to the country this evening, but I preferred staying at home to perform the pleasant duty of writing to you, my dear Wash.

You ask me to write long letters, and O! how gladly would I do so, were I *allowed*, but the letter examiner, whoever he is, for fear that I should gratify your request, wrote on the back of the letter "long letters not delivered—examiner." I am so glad to hear you are so much better. I wrote last week, and directed to the hospital, but fear you will not receive the letter. How I wish you could be here now to enjoy strawberries. I never put one in my mouth that I do not think of *you*, and other friends.

The country now is beautiful, but I can't enjoy it. There is so much sorrow and suffering in the land. Do you remember Mr. Christian, who taught at Airwell?[18] He was killed in the last fight. Poor Phil! Was so devoted to him, He will be so lonely even if *he* is spared. Fannie is very uneasy about him. She sends her love, and says "tell him, I *reckon*." I suppose you will understand what she means by that. The times here are hard. O! for an end to this *cruel, cruel* war! We have not heard from Hanover for a long time. Cousin Randolph has a little girl Lizzie Randolph. Cousin Wm. P. has returned from his second trip to Georgia. All send love. Faithfully yrs

M—

16. Phillip Meade Nelson enlisted in Company D, 3rd Virginia Cavalry on May 3, 1862, as a private. He was wounded once on July 9, 1863, at Funkstown, Md., ACWRD.

17. Here Mollie refers to more than just the prison censors, as family members usually read letters such as the ones between Mollie and Wash.

18. Located in Hanover County, Va.

James W. Myers is at Pt. Lookout. He is a first coz of Fannie. His mother
is very uneasy about him.[19]

Officers Camp, Point Lookout, June 7, 1864

As I foretold in my last letter to you, dearest Mollie, I have been moved
from the hospital to the Camp—and indeed, I have so entirely recovered
that I am not even considered a fit subject for a hospital tent, but allowed
to "rough it" with the best of us. I like the change—it is pleasant to have
no bottles of physic around, no doctors whispering about you. I even enjoy such a night as I have just spent, rain driving through the tent, wind
blowing under it, every now & then a rope or a peg giving away, making
it necessary for some one to go out & fix it, and thus get the full benefit
of wind & rain. I like it because it reminds me of other tents I have been
in, of the other winds & rain I have gone through, or rather, which have
gone through me. I am thus explicit, that I may convince you of my entire
recovery. There is one thing that troubles me very seriously, and it is the
only reason I regret leaving the Hospital, and that is, I had just begun
to get letters from you, and now, as has always been the case in every
change of place I have made heretofore, I may have to go a month or six
weeks without hearing from you. And thus, my darling, in the hardest
trial that can be put upon us, I doubt whether you have an idea of the
influence you exercise over me, and of the value I place upon every line
from you—Well, I won't talk about this now. I will wait for better times,
when no eyes but yours will see what I write, or, better still, when I can tell
your ear about all I have felt. I have met with two countrymen, who were
captured in the late fight, they could give me no news from home, except
that all were well. You don't know them. All my efforts to find Everard
Meade have been unsuccessful. Are you sure he was sent to Point Lookout? George Byrd[20] of Baltimore wrote me a very kind letter the other

---

19. Postscript written in pen upside down on the top of the letter. James W. Myers, a
clerk, enlisted as a private in the 2nd Virginia Infantry at Charlestown, Va., in 1861. He was
wounded in 1862 at Cedar Run, Va., and captured at Spotsylvania Court House on May 12,
1864. He was imprisoned at Point Lookout, Md., and later Elmira, N.Y. He was exchanged
on March 2, 1865. Entry for James W. Myers, ACWRD.

20. George H. Byrd was a merchant in Baltimore. In 1860 he lived with Rachel Boston,
a mulatto woman. Although regulations sometimes prohibited importation of goods and
money, prisoners with outside connections frequently received such items. As a haven of
southern sympathizers, Baltimore was a common source of funds and supplies. 1860 U.S.

day. He enclosed a check, which was very acceptable as I had left all my funds with Lt. Randolph. Cousin Lou[21] & child were well, staying out in the country. We are ordered to inform correspondents that letters over a page long, will not be allowed. I fear you will think me changeable, after what I told you in my last letter. I was in the Hospital then & had not seen this order. Whenever you see your sister Anne always give her my love. I covet a brothers place in her affections. May I trust my interest in your hands? Love to all. God bless you, my darling. Your devoted

Wash Nelson

Officers Camp Point Lookout June 12 1864

I was most agreeably surprised yesterday evening, dearest, by your letter of the 6th. Judging from experience, I supposed my change of place from the Hospital to the camp would interrupt, for some time, our communication. I will take great pleasure in trying to find out James W. Myers. I could do so much better if I know the number of his regiment. I understand that Channing Page[22] is a prisoner—taken in the fight at Spotsylvania C. H. I would like very much to see him—I left him in my tent on the 15th of last October, and this is the first I have heard of him since. Had you heard that Willie Randolph was killed? I have, so far, heard from only two of my Hanover friends, the Cookes;[23] both of them are safe. I have

---

Census, Baltimore, Maryland, Ward 20, population schedule, p. 14, dwelling 80, family 86, George H. Byrd; digital image, *Ancestry.com* (http://wwww.ancestry.com : accessed April 24, 2017); citing NARA microfilm publication M653, roll 466.

21. Lucy C. Byrd and her child, Anna H. Byrd lived with Rachel Boston and George H. Byrd in Baltimore. 1860 U.S. Census, Baltimore, Md., pop. Sch., p. 14, dwell. 80, fam. 86, George H. Byrd.

22. Probably Richard Channing Moore Page (1841–98) of Albemarle County, Va. Moore was a sergeant in the 1st Virginia Light Artillery from Rockbridge County. He was wounded at Gettysburg in 1863, captured in February 1864, and almost immediately escaped. See entry for Richard Channing Moore Page, ACWRD. Also see "Civil War Soldier Records and Profiles, 1861–65," database, *Ancestry.com* (http://ancestry.com : accessed April 24, 2017), entry for Richard Channing Moore Page; citing "The Virginia Regimental Histories Series."

23. James C. and John M. Cooke, sons of John Cooke, an Episcopal minister in Hanover County, Va. 1860 U.S. Census, Hanover County, Virginia, population schedule, Upper Revenue District, p. 460 (stamped), dwelling 319, family 315, John C., John M., and John Cooke; digital image, *Ancestry.com* (http://ancestry.com : accessed April 25, 2017); citing NARA microfilm publication M653, roll 1350.

tried in vain to hear anything about "Uncle Buck."[24] God grant that his dear red head may be safe & sound. I remember young Christian[25] very well; was he in Phil's Company? Give my love to Fannie. Tell her I am very much obliged for that "I reckon". It is an epigrammatic mode of expression peculiar to herself. I shall give it a voluminous interpretation. I can well believe how gloriously beautiful your lovely country is just now. It grieves me, my love that you can't enjoy it. It is true that viewed only in the light of contrast, nature, with its beautiful garb, its sweet fragrance and its soft melodies, seems to mock the broken hearted sorrowing of the land. But look upon it, dearest, as the bow of promise, as the type of peace, sent by the Almighty, for our comfort, to let us know that *He* still ruleth, and that all *will* be well, and you will enjoy its beauties & be comforted by them. You speak of the hardness of the times—I trust you do not speak from experience—tell me, my beloved, has any want come to *you?* Tell me your sorrows, let me at least share with you the knowledge of them. You know that I love you better than my own life, grant me then the privilege of comforting you with words of love. Alas, that I can do no more. I suppose you have gotten my last letter by this time, and know that I am perfectly well—in fact I am now such a prodigy of health & strength that I have been elected to the post of instructor of gymnasticks. You would be amused to see how I make the fellows twist themselves out of shape every evening. Love to all. God bless you my darling.

> Your devoted
> Wash

Officers Camp Point Lookout June 14 1864

Your letter of June 3rd has just reached me, my darling Mollie; it came via the Hospital, which accounts for its being behind yours of the 6th. You ask why I have not been exchanged. I must confess my inability to answer

24. Possibly Berkley Minor, whom Wash describes as a redhead in his letter to Mollie, October 31, 1864 (see chap. 3).

25. Heath Jones Christian Jr. grew up near Richmond. He enlisted as a private in the 3rd Virginia Cavalry in 1862 at the age of seventeen or eighteen. He died at Todd's Tavern, Va., on May 7, 1864. ACWRD; citing NARA microfilm publication M324, no roll number, "Compiled Service Records of Confederate Soldiers Who Served in Organizations from the State of Virginia," 3rd Cavalry (2nd Virginia Cavalry); 1860 U.S. Census, Henrico County, Va., population schedule, Western Subdivision, p. 1019 (stamped), dwelling 1065, family 1053, H. J. Christian; digital image, *Ancestry.com* (http://ancestry.com : accessed April 25, 2017); citing NARA microfilm publication M653, roll 1353.

you. I can assure you the fault is not on my side. I have never been too sick for it, at least I never considered myself so, though I believe I would cry onward to "Dixie" if I were in the very jaws of the "Grim Monster."[26] I have no right to complain because I did not get off, for there are several here now who were captured three of four months before I was. I am not at all disheartened. My time will come one of these days. Meanwhile if I can only keep the health & spirits I have now, there are few things [that] can hurt me. I don't fear the future the least bit—have scarcely any anxiety about it. It does concern me though to learn that you, my precious one, have been sick, and your announcing in the same sentence that you are so much better, is an inexpressible relief. Are you sure, dearest, that you *really* are *so much* better, and were not influenced by the desire not to make me uneasy about you? I heard from Lt. R.[27] about four days ago—he had been sick with chills & fever, & was just out of the Hospital, but wrote that he was "all right" again; and in proof of it gave me an account of a game of "Baseball" he had just played. In his letter he begged me to let him know if I had heard anything of his brother; it was a sad duty to tell him of his death, which I learned from an officer taken where he was killed. Poor Tom—he was dreading something of the kind when I left him—he had not heard from home for a long time, and wondered why they didn't write. I expect you acted wisely in not sending Jennie's letter with yours. Send it to me, and add a sentence from yourself that I may have something from you both at once. It will give me great pleasure to send your love to Mrs. Massie. I owe her a great deal—she won't *let* me want for anything. My own sister wouldn't be kinder. She has told me so much about her little "blue eyed daughter" that I begged her to send me the "little beauty's["] photograph. I have not received a reply as yet. Don't fear, my darling, that I will think your letters cold. I fully appreciate the difficulty under which they are written—and even without the knowledge of this difficulty, I could not think anything cold which assured me that you were "faithfully" mine. Continue to write as you have been doing, dearest, and I will never complain that my cup of happiness is lacking. God bless you—my dear own dearest love.

Love to all Your devoted
Wash

I send ½ a dozen stamps

Mollie wrote the following note on the back of a short letter from Wash's sister, Jennie. While the note is dated June 14, 1864, Jennie's letter is dated March 13,

---

26. A literary allusion for Death
27. Lieutenant Thomas Randolph.

1864. In the letter—the fifth she claimed to have sent to Wash while he was impris-
oned at Johnson's Island—Jennie explained that the scrutiny of censors "chill[ed]"
her ideas. She asked Wash for news about friends who might have been imprisoned
with Wash, reported that all was well at home, and conveyed her love.[28]

June 14 1864

I am afraid you will think me selfish my dear Wash for not having sent this
letter before, and really I must confess I have been, for every opportunity
I had of mailing a letter, I felt as if I must write myself, and I feared to
send it with mine lest both should be lost. I shall write again as soon as I
hear from you. All send love.

    Yrs as ever

    M. N. S.

"Home" June 17 1864

My dear Wash

    Your letter of the 7th reached me yesterday. I had not heard from you
before for nearly two weeks, and I had almost again begun to hope that
you were exchanged. I do not hear from you as often now, as I did when
you were further off. So you have met with another kind friend. You
have indeed been fortunate. Much more so than *I* expected. I believe I
never told you that Everard has been exchanged. Robert P[29] wrote that
he had seen him in Richmond. We heard from Long Branch the other
day. Hugh is going about on crutches. He has a foot,[30] but cannot wear
it yet a while. Old Clip is as *dull* as possible. I have been reading some of
Grace Aguilar's[31] works lately, which have served to pass away time quite
pleasantly. Our Sunday School has opened again. I have a class of boys

---

28. Jennie to Wash, March 13, 1854, box 2, folder 13, Nelson Family Papers Ms1989-021,
Special Collections, Virginia Tech, Blacksburg, Va. The other four letters that Jennie sent
to Wash are missing.

29. Possibly Robert Page, a cousin.

30. A prosthetic limb.

31. Grace Aguilar, an early nineteenth-century British writer. Many of her works were
published posthumously after her death at age thirty-one in 1847. Richmond, Va., newspapers advertised her books into the 1850s. See "Choice of New Books at the Exchange
Bookstore," *Daily Dispatch* (Richmond, Va.), June 21, 1852, 4.

between the ages of 15 and 17. They study questions on "Acts." Would rather have had a class of smaller boys and given these to some more experienced teacher, but they preferred coming to me, so I did not like to refuse. Have you heard from home since your removal and do they know of the change? Coz. F.[32] is owing me a letter, but I intend writing again soon. Are they still exchanging? I hear not. God bless and shield you from harm prays

Your devoted M—

Officers Camp
Point Lookout June 22 1864

Somehow or other I expected a letter from you to day, my darling Mollie, and I feel as much disappointed in not getting one, as if it had been promised me. Well, I must do the next most pleasant thing, viz: write to you. I hear of some of my old friends, nearly every day, from prisoners that come in. Dick Page[33] & Wellford Corbin[34] are here; they were captured near Petersburg the 15th of this month. Dick reports Cousin Posey[35] safe & sound up to the hour of his capture. Do you know whether or not Wellford Corbin's wife is dead? I am under the impression I heard of her death last winter, so I have not asked him anything about her. All my efforts to trace up young Myers have so far been failures, though he may very possibly be in the next Camp, and I never find him out.[36] Whenever I am so fortunate I will write you word. We see the papers every day—they are eagerly read as you may suppose—Some of the journals are as amusing as "The Budget of Fun"[37]—such splendid caricatures.

---

32. Most likely Cousin Fannie, though Mollie's script is rather unclear here.

33. Richard Mann Page, born in Greenway, Va., in 1837, enlisted in the 26th Virginia Infantry in 1861. He was captured at Petersburg on June 15, 1864, and imprisoned at Point Lookout, Md., and Fort Delaware until June 14, 1865. Entry for Richard Mann Page, ACWRD.

34. S. Welford Corbin. While a prisoner at Point Lookout, S. Wellford Corbin sent his sister tobacco tags, which were donated to the Museum of the Confederacy. *Catalogue of the Confederate Museum, Twelfth and Clay Streets, Richmond, VA.* (Richmond, Va.: I. N. Jones Print, 1898), 26.

35. Powhatan Robertson "Posey" Page enlisted on May 1, 1861, as the captain of Company F, 26th Virginia Infantry. He died at Taylor's Farm, Va., in 1864, two days after Dick Page last saw him. Entry for Powhatan Robertson Page, ACWRD.

36. Myers was in fact imprisoned at Point Lookout.

37. *Frank Leslie's Budget of Fun* was one of many popular illustrated periodicals that capitalized on increased readership during the Civil War. See Alice Fahs, *The Imagined Civil*

Were I the intimate friend of the Editors, I would advise them to set up a rival "Punch" establishment. Their success under that head is a foregone conclusion.[38]

Rumors are current among the prisoners that we are about to make another change of "base"; some say only to another prison, and others contend then an exchange is the programme. Judging from experience and the present status of things, my own private opinion is, that we won't get to Richmond this trip either. By the time we *do* reach "Dixie", we will be quite "travelled," I confess our looks may not warrant the word, "gentlemen." Every move is an interest to me, not as it concerns my personal comfort, I never did care much about that, but as regards its bearing upon my communication with you, my beloved.

I *do dread* having to pass whole weeks without a single letter from you. Therefore, unless my more sanguine friends are right in their exchange surmise, I would very much prefer staying where I am. If you should not hear from me again for sometime, don't think me sick. Dick Page has just come in my tent. He knows, to whom I am writing, collectively, but not the individual. He sends his best love to all. Does Miss Lily Dandridge ever speak of Brig. Genl. Dearing?[39] Love to all. God bless you my darling.

Your devoted Wash Nelson

June 22 1864

My Dear Wash,

My heart was gladdened yesterday by the receipt of two of your *dear* letters. Accept my thanks for the stamps. Although I had just succeeded in getting some, yours are very well acceptable, and will enable me to write oftener. I hope you did not rob yourself. It seems contrary to the *"rules of warfare"* that a *poor* prisoner should send stamps to a correspondent. I am glad to hear that your health is so good now, and trust it may continue. *Do* remember, when taking gymnastic exercises that somebody

---

War: Popular Literature of the North and South, 1861–1865 (Chapel Hill: University of North Carolina Press, 2003), 56.

38. While *Budget of Fun* was popular, American readers were also familiar with the British humor-based publications, one of the more famous being Henry Mayhew's and Ebenezer Landells's *Punch*, based in London.

39. Dearing had been promoted to brigadier general in May 1864.

is interested in the preservation of your body in a sound condition. H, and Aunt F. were at Mr. Pendleton's a few days ago, and heard cheering letters from the two boys. Cousin Hugh has not returned yet. I believe I never told you of cousin Tom Nelson's death.[40] His daughter Mary[41] is engaged to a Lt. Oliver from Md.[42] A perfect stranger. I am sorry to hear of Lt. Randolph's illness. If you will tell him to send his Mother a letter to my address, I will contrive it to her. I have at last succeeded in finding out Mrs. D's name. You should direct your letter to Mrs Rebecca or Mrs. John B. Dangerfield. I fear I have kept you waiting a long time. I sent cousin Jennie's letter some days ago. Did you ever get it.

You misunderstood my allusion to the hard times. We have not suffered at all in comparison with many others. I hear that Hickory Hill[43] is torn to pieces. All send love. Yrs with warmest love

M—

James Myers belongs to the 2nd Va. Co. A

June 26th 1864

My dear Wash

Although I have written so recently, as I hear of an opportunity to the depot, I will send you a few lines of love, fearing I may not have another for sometime. I fear you suffer much this warm weather; should think the confinement must be terrible. I am glad to hear of the Cookes. We have not been able to learn anything of Berkeley. Don't you remember

---

40. Thomas F. Nelson lived in Clarke County, Va., in 1850. He died April 9, 1864. 1850 U.S. Census, Clarke County, Virginia, population schedule, 12th District, p. 203B, dwelling 505, family 505, Thomas F. Nelson; digital image, *Ancestry.com* (http://ancestry.com : accessed April 25, 2017); citing NARA microfilm publication M432, roll 940.

41. Mary Nelson, aged nineteen in 1860, lived in Nelson County, Va., on a large farm with her father, Thomas F. Nelson. Mary Nelson was born in Clarke County, Va. 1860 U.S. Census, Nelson County, Virginia, population schedule, p. 719 (stamped), dwelling 227, family 227, Mary Nelson; digital image, *Ancestry.com* (http://ancestry.com : accessed April 25, 2017); citing NARA microfilm publication M653, roll 1365.

42. Possibly James Oliver, who enlisted as a corporal in the 1st Battalion Maryland Cavalry. ACWRD.

43. Hickory Hill was a plantation in Hanover County, Va., in the vicinity of Wash's home. It was the home of Williams Carter Wickham, a distinguished statesman, businessman, and—at this time—Confederate cavalry commander. Hickory Hill, Hanover County, Va., Nomination to the National Register of Historic Places, 1974, on *Virginia Department of Historic Resources* website, http://www.dhr.virginia.gov/registers/Counties/Hanover /042-0100_Hickory_Hill_1974_Final_Nomination.pdf.

how happy we all were together this time last year? We spend our time
thinking and talking over what happened on each day. But how many,
who were then full of life and joy, are now under the sod. O! For an end
to this shedding of blood. It is inhuman. Aunt Fanny wrote to Lt. R. tell
him when you write. All send love. Ever yours.

 M—

Fort Delaware June 28 1864

If my last letter has reached you, my darling Mollie, you see by the above
that I was a true prophet. I had hardly mailed my letter when we received
orders to start. And in due course of time arrived at this place and here
we are safe enough. I told you I had heard from Cousin Posey through
Dick Page, up to June 15th. I was very much grieved on coming here to
hear that he was killed on the 17th and I fear there is little room to doubt
the truth of the report. It comes from an officer of his brigade captured
after the 17th. I am so sorry, my darling, that the little short letters I write
you should ever contain bad news. But you know the love which prompts
me to tell you all the truth, and will, I trust, feel the less pain because
you know that I sympathize with you in your loss & share with you your
sorrow.

Do you remember a request I made you, while at Point Lookout, and
your reply that you would gladly comply with it but for a certain addition
to the letter? I think I can test now whether you were earnest for as far as
I can judge that objection no longer exists.[44] Try, dearest, you know what
infinite pleasure you will give me. I found two old college friends here
waiting to meet me. One was Rodes Massie,[45] you have heard me speak
of him. My respect and admiration for him are very much increased,
since he has shown himself the sensible man, I thought him, by getting

---

44. Wash refers to the inconsistency of prison censors. At Point Lookout, he requested
Mollie write him longer letters, but she demurred, explaining that the prison censor had
written a harsh line on an undelivered letter.

45. D. Rodes Massie was born in Waynesboro, Va., and attended the University of Virginia with Wash. He enlisted as a corporal in the Charlottesville Light Artillery on March
20, 1862, and was promoted June 25, 1863. Massie was furloughed on October 30, 1863,
hospitalized on December 1, 1863, and reported as a prisoner of war May 12, 1864, at Spotsylvania Court House. He was exchanged December 15, 1864. He was hospitalized on May
22, 1864, for chronic bronchitis. After the war he was a professor at Washington College
and Richmond College. Graham T. Dozier, ed., *A Gunner in Lee's Army: The Civil War Letters
of Thomas Henry Carter* (Chapel Hill: University of North Carolina Press, 2014), 287n6.

married. He tells me he has the best wife, and the sweetest wife that ever existed. I tell him I have no doubt of the truth of his statement as to the wives that *have been*. I was delighted to learn from him that "Uncle Buck" has a position in the Engineer Corps. It is such a relief to hear of his promotion in some other than a heavenly line—an unchristianlike looking sentiment—but I couldn't bear to hear that the dear old red head was under the sod. When you write direct to me at Fort Delaware. Division 36. Love to all. May God bless & preserve you, my beloved.

Your devoted Wash—

Prisoner of War
Fort Delaware
Division 36
Fort Delaware July 11 1864

Jennie's letter has been received at last, my darling Mollie; you need not accuse yourself of selfishness for not sending it before—if it was selfishness, it is so flattering to me that I can only admire the sentiment, and love more dearly, if that be possible, one who expresses it so sweetly. You said in one of your late letters that you didn't hear from me as often as when I was farther off—indeed, my love, the fault is not mine. I have written very often, even when I thought there was little chance of my letters going. I know you have not blamed me for this; you know too well the depths of my heart to believe that I could let pass any chance of sending the little notes, that are permitted. Why, my beloved, the dearest pleasure of my life, is exchanging with you, as often as I dare, some few words— meaningless, almost, but for the heart that interprets them. O! It is hard to feel so much, and yet express so little, and even that little frozen by the idea of the ordeal it must pass. I would make a poor letter examiner; the first glance at an epistle to a very dear one, would so move my heart with remembrance of its own anguish at the idea of the publicity about to be given to its dearest arcana, that pity & sympathy would triumph over duty, and the missive allowed to reach its fair reader, undesecrated by my eyes. I accept your caution, in regard to gymnastics. That you wish it, is reason enough for me to take care of myself. Just now, however, all exercise is out of the question; I think the sun has been trying himself—just to see whether there is any limit to the supply of heat. All we ask is that he will not overwhelm us with proofs of his power; we are ready to accord to him credit for an infinite amount and we are good judges, for we

Letter from Wash to Mollie, July 11, 1864. Box 2, folder 31, Nelson Family Papers, Ms1989-021, Special Collections, Virginia Tech, Blacksburg, Va.

have not green trees, with cool breezes blowing beneath, to distract our attention from the *great* mass of heat about us. I have been finding pleasure & employment lately in a game of whist. Our object is to pass time pleasantly and at the same time not to let the mind become a dead letter. And I assure you, a game of whist between four good players goes a long way towards this end. I don't think Aunt Judy even, could she appreciate the circumstances, would object to this; please tell me what *you* think of the game. I ask your opinion not because I feel the need of an excuse for the practice, but because your views on every subject are dear to me, & I love to have them. I feel communication is not very open between us now. God bless you, my precious one. Love to all.

Your devoted Wash

Fort Pulaski Ga October 31st 1864

O for a letter from you, my darling, is the burden of my song, and has been for some months, but I know it is not your fault that I don't hear from you. I doubt whether you have any idea where I am.

I wrote shortly before leaving Morris Island, and inclosed to my sister, hoping to get a letter to you in some way. Our prospects are better in every respect here than at Morris Island,[46] and I even hope we may again receive each other's letters regularly. I had very little idea, when leaving Johnson's Island for Dixie on the 22nd of April, that the 31st of October would find me in Fort Pulaski Ga. It does seem impossible for me to be exchanged; no matter how fair a start I make, there is always some Jonah[47] in the party to stop the whole business. Well; I am hopeful still, thank God, looking to what the next month or two may do for me. Who knows, I may *see you* by Christmas yet! How my heart beats at the very thought and now I feel like putting my pen down and dreaming over the sweet pictures the idea calls up. In spite of all I have been through since this time a year ago, I can hardly regret my imprisonment, because it has shown me, more thoroughly than perhaps I ever could have learned under other circumstances, how completely my heart is yours; the fruit of this knowledge will be unmeasured happiness in the years which will, I trust, be granted us together, no matter what our circumstances. To be

46. Morris Island is a small sandy island east of Charleston near Fort Sumter and most known for being the site of the Confederate garrison, Battery Wagner. After Union forces captured Battery Wagner, it became the site where Confederate prisoners selected for retaliation were placed in late summer and early fall of 1864.

47. In the nineteenth century, this was slang for "bad luck." Jonah was a minor prophet of the Hebrew Bible, whom God ordered to prophesy at a town called Nineveh, but Jonah rejected God's call. As he sailed away from Nineveh, a storm threw Jonah into the sea and he was swallowed whole by a huge fish or whale. Jonah sat in the belly of the whale for three days before he decided to accept God's command and return to preach to the Ninevites. Jonah 1:4.

able to say "My beloved is mine, and I am my beloved's,"[48] and to say it with the whole heart is the fullest cup of happiness to be found on earth. Have you thought hardly, because you have not heard from me for so long? Jennie writes that your last letter from me was more than three months ago. Your happiness is my first object, and when ever I let any length of time pass without writing, it was to spare you uneasiness. Trust me fully, my own love; you may safely do so, for I have neither the will nor the power to break a single trust; your influence with me is "the power behind the throne greater than the throne." The constant stir in your part of the country keeps me mighty uneasy, and the absence of all news from you during it all is mighty hard to bear. May God shield you and yours.

I was most agreeably surprised a few days ago by a letter from Berkeley M.[49] The first I have heard of him for the longest. The old bird writes like himself. Was flourishing his dear red head about his native Edgewood, being on furlough. What do you think of his complaining of this state of single blessedness, and mourning that he couldn't "*afford*" to change it? I have a notion to cane him on sight for such an expression.

Best love to all. Remember I am aching to hear from you. God bless you my precious one.

Your devoted Wash Nelson

---

48. Song of Solomon 6:3.

49. Most likely Carter Nelson Berkeley Minor (1842–1930) of Edgewood, in Hanover County, Va. The son of Lucius Horatio Minor, "Berkeley" enlisted in the Rockbridge (Va.) 1st Light Artillery on November 16, 1861, was promoted sergeant on November 3, 1863, and was promoted second lieutenant on November 7, 1864. Prior to enlisting, Minor was a student and a member of the same fraternity as Wash Nelson (Delta Kappa Epsilon) at the University of Virginia. "U.S., School Catalogs, 1765–1935," database, *Ancestry.com*; "U.S., Civil War Soldier Records and Profiles, 1861–1865," database, *Historical Data Systems*, comp.

CHAPTER 4

Early Spring 1865

Silence and Anxiety

What Wash and Mollie felt and experienced after Wash's final letter from Fort Pulaski on Halloween Day, 1864, is difficult to know for sure. Indeed, Wash's removal to Morris Island and Fort Pulaski made it more difficult to send and receive letters. While the reason for this difficulty is unclear, letters leaving prisons were likely more restricted because there was no land route for mail transportation. It is also possible that part of the retaliation included stricter mail regulations. While the causes were uncertain, the results were not: Wash and Mollie exchanged no letters for months. In the void, they read and reread old letters and attempted to interpret the meaning of the silence between each other. This cycle of silence and anxiety becomes clear, however, in the letters they received the following spring.

Fort Delaware March 13th 1865

My darling Mollie, I arrived here from Fort Pulaski yesterday, have just seen Dick Page, imagine my joy at learning that the mail rout[e] to you is open. I tried until there was no use in trying to communicate with you. I wonder if you have given me credit for the efforts I have made to get letters to you, and for the trouble I have been in for fear you wouldn't get them & wouldn't know what to think of me? I assure you this has been my greatest trial. Bodily suffering weighs little when the great hopes of the heart is in the balance.

I have heard of you now & then, through Jennie & other friends, as being well, and in her last Jennie sent me a scrap of one of your letters to her. The hand writing & the name by themselves are treasure to me.

We left Pulaski expecting to land at City Point but, with such a Jonah[1] as myself along the party might have known we would stop at Delaware or some such safe place. Well I suppose I will be exchanged one of these days. Sometimes I think if I were one of those generous people we read about in books, I would write to you not to waste your youth & beauty on me, but, my own love, I can't find any where in my heart, so selfish is it, any such inclination. As soon as I get fixed here again, get some big paper[,] stamps &c, I shall write to you to make up for lost time, won't you second me? Best love to all. May God bless you dearest. Your devoted
Wash Nelson

"Home" March 21st 1865

My dear Wash—Imagine if you can, my surprise at receiving a few minutes ago a letter from Fort Del. directed in your well-known hand writing. I thought I *must* be mistaken, until I opened it, and found that it was actually from *yourself.* Really the Fates seem to be against your being exchanged. How often have I pictured to myself your arrival at home, and the joy of the loved ones to have you with them again. Little did I think that when next I heard from you, you would be back in Fort. Del. But I suppose we must be patient; one thing we know they cannot hold you forever. Until a few days ago, it had been five months since I had heard one word from you. O! how my heart has ached for only one line, to tell me you were well. We heard from cousin Jennie and Frank,[2] but I reckon you have had later news. They told of cousin Betsy Nelson's[3] death, and

---

1. In the previous chapter, Wash wrote there must be some Jonah among the prisoners because every time they thought they were going home, they ended up in some other prison. Here, in 1865, he returns to that biblical allusion but concludes that he himself is the Jonah.

2. Frank Nelson was Wash's younger half-brother. According to the 1860 Federal Census, Frank would have been fourteen years old in 1865. 1860 U.S. Census, Hanover County, Va., population schedule, Upper Revenue District, dwelling 222, family 219, p. 448 (stamped), Frank Nelson; digital image, *Ancestry.com* (http://ancestry.com : accessed April 25, 2017); citing NARA microfilm publication M653, roll 1350.

3. Possibly Elizabeth Page Nelson, who lived with Philip M. Nelson in Clarke County. 1860 U.S. Census, Clarke County, Va., population schedule, Millwood, dwelling 505, family 482, p. 667 (stamped), Philip M. Nelson, Betsey Nelson; digital image, *Ancestry.com* (http://ancestry.com : accessed April 22, 2017); citing NARA microfilm publication M653, roll 1341. Betsey Nelson died on February 8, 1865. *Ancestry. com* (accessed April 22, 2017); citing *Find A Grave,* http://www.findagrave.com/cgi-bin/fg.cgi.

of C. Cookes marriage the 16th and Willie Meade's[4] the 17th of this month. So much has happened since I last wrote, and I have got so much to tell, that I hardly know what to say first. I have been corresponding all winter with a soldier at Fort Del. He belongs to Div 33, Lt. Haymaker,[5] so you can make his acquaintance if you choose, and let me know what you think of him. As he is a stranger to me, I am unable to give any opinion. How we became correspondents, I have not room to tell just now. Cousin Jennie says it is the "Verdict of all Dixie" that I ought to be there in view of the gen[l] exchange now going on. Let me know whether you will be at Fort Del any length of time, as I have some little things to send you by mail. If you want money I can send it in small quantities. How has your health stood the long confinement? All send quantities of love to you. May God bless you, and answer my prayers for your safe return home. Write often. Faithfully and devotedly yours

Mollie

I send some stamps

"Home" March 24th 1865

My Dear Wash, I wrote you a short letter a day or two ago, but judging you by myself, I think you will not object to reading another so soon. I cannot express my joy at hearing from you again. Am so proud of my letter, that I have not been able to think of anything else since it came, and I don't suppose I could count the times that I have read it over. During the Winter, when I was unable to hear from you, sometimes I used to get so low spirited, that I would take my writing desk, and read over all your letters, until I have become perfectly familiar with each one. Now, I hope, I shall have some new ones. What have you been doing with yourself all this *long, long* time? How have you managed to pass away

4. Possibly James C. Cooke, or another relation of the Cookes of Hanover County, Va., whom Wash mentioned in the letter to Mollie dated June 12, 1864 (see chap. 3). Willie Meade likely refers to William T. Meade of Clarke County, Va., who married Nannie B. Winston in March 1865. See "Virginia Select Marriages, 1785–1940," database, *Ancestry.com* (http://ancestry.com : accessed on April 26, 2017), entry for Nannie B. Winston, March 9, 1865, Louisa, Va.; citing *Virginia, Select Marriages, 1785–1940.*" Also see "Sir John Randolph and His Descendants, Continued," *Times Dispatch* (Richmond, Va.), July 19, 1914, 9.

5. James W. Haymaker, of Montgomery County, Md., enlisted in the 4th Virginia Infantry in 1861 and was captured September 22, 1864, at Fisher's Hill, Va. He was released from Fort Delaware on May 10, 1865, record for James W. Haymaker (Confederate), ACWRD.

the dreary hours of eighteen months imprisonment? Little did we think when we parted that you would have to endure such a series of trials and hardships. Though I could not hear from you my thoughts were with you constantly, and I have not thought of bestowing my *"youth and beauty"* upon any other soldier, so your generosity, is not likely to be put to the test *yet a while.* I don't know what *might* happen *if you don't get out of prison before the Summer is over.*

At present I don't suppose anyone would like to be burdened with such a *poor old cripple.* About three weeks ago, I got a fall and sprained my knee, which has caused me a good deal of pain, as well as inconvenience. For a week I could not put my foot to the floor at all, but I am a great deal better now, can walk very well with a slight limp. So you need not be afraid of being compelled to *lead me through life.* I read a great deal last Winter, and in that way managed to keep my time so fully occupied that the lonely months slipped away rapidly, and now spring has opened, bringing with it bright hopes to cheer our sad hearts. I don't think I ever enjoyed a spring as much as I have this. We have had such sweet weather lately and the country, tho terribly devastated is still beautiful. *Your friends* have been very accommodating to allow you to spend the Winter in the south, and then take you north as the Summer season approaches.[6] I trust however you are not destined to remain a captive much longer. We saw Cope last Summer for a few hours. He is the same *old thing,* and was delighted to see us, spoke most affectionately of you, as did all the other boys. Did you ever hear anything of Mr. Dunlap's engagement to Mrs. Harrison?[7] Cousin Jennie mentioned something of the kind some time ago. I was afraid to tease him, he is so dignified. Phil was here, but of course I did not see much of him. Himself and his "Bright particular"[8] made all things straight, and seemed to be *very* happy together. She has not heard from him very lately. Aunt Betsey[9] expects to go to housekeeping next week. They will live in the house that Mr. Myers now occu-

---

6. As in her letter to Wash from spring 1864, Mollie avoids talking directly about military affairs. This time she substitutes "friends" for the U.S. Army and "Summer season" for the anticipated military campaign.

7. Probably Mollie's cousin, Nannie Harrison, whom Wash mentions in the letter dated April 2, 1865.

8. William Shakespeare, *All's Well that Ends Well,* act 1, scene 1.

9. May refer to Elizabeth Burwell Nelson (1824–1912), who married John Page in 1847. Richard Channing Moore Page, *Genealogy of the Page Family in Virginia. Also a Condensed Account of the Nelson, Walker, Pendelton and Randolph Families* (New York: Press of the Publishers' Printing Co., 1893), 182.

pies.[10] They stand their losses wonderfully, but of course are delighted at the thought of once having a home of their own. Mrs. Hank wishes to know if you have heard anything of Lt. Newman. Has Lt. Randolph been exchanged? I suppose you know he has lost another brother. I am anxiously looking for another letter tomorrow. Hope I may not be disappointed. I wish there was no War in the land, and you were here this evening, would we not be *happy*. Fondly yours

Mollie

I send with this a package containing a pr socks, 2 collars, a [illeg.] and a cravat.

Division 34 Fort Delaware March 31st 1865

Two letters and a package, all from you, my darling Mollie, made me so happy this morning that I hardly remember that I am yet a prisoner; to find you still, my own darling, after not having heard from you for so long, is such sweet comfort, not that I ever doubted you, I think I would die if I did that, but then to have again your own true word for it is joy indeed.

I am so sorry you won't get a letter from me as soon as you expect. I was so completely out of everything on getting here, that I had to beg the materials for the one I wrote, and begging being something I have not yet learned to do with a good grace, I determined to wait until I received assistance from some of my friends—that has come, and now I am ready & *able* to write whenever I will, so after the receipt of this, you needn't expect long intervals between my letters. The articles you sent me are very acceptable on their own account, and *you* know how I value them for the sender's sake: they fit & suit me exactly. I must tell you, not to risk anything more to me by mail; this was given me with the express understanding that all packages sent by mail would in future be confiscated. I am so delighted at receiving *this* token from my beloved, that I don't

---

10. Most likely John Myers (b. ca. 1820), who in 1860 was a forty-year-old "farm labourer," living in Middleway with his five children, including John W. Myers named in Mollie and Wash's 1864 correspondence (see chap. 3). 1860 U.S. Census, Jefferson County, W.Va., population schedule, Charles Town Post Office, p. 892 (stamped), dwelling 287, family 276, John Myers, digital image, *Ancestry.com* (http://ancestry.com : accessed April 26, 2017); citing NARA microfilm publication M324, 653, roll 1355.

bother about the future, All I ask or wish of the mail is that it will bring me *very often* such sweet letters as I got this morning.

I am so sorry that you should have been suffering pain; do you remember your caution to me last summer about gymnastic exercises? The sequel has proved that *I* ought to have been mentor. I am truly glad you are so much better, to know you suffer is the worst pain I can have. I don't *fear* having to "lead you through life," and if I did, all my sorrow would be for you. *I* would be all the happier at having you so entirely dependent upon me; you couldn't leave me for somebody else then, as you so *wickedly* threaten in case I don't get out of prison this summer. When you find him, clothe him in tripple "oak & brass,"[11] for I shall then believe I was born to be hung, and shan't be slow to fulfill my destiny. You ask how I have been and how I managed to pass away the time. I have not been really sick since I left here last August. I had a touch of scurvy, but I determined I would not give up to it, and a kind Providence enabled me to stave it off. Many of our poor fellows who are now dead, would, I believe, be with us now, if they had had more strength of will. I passed the time, while it was daylight, in reading, playing chess, whist, &c. And when the long evening came, I used to button my great coat up, pull the cape over my head, and treat myself to a long, sweet interview with thought & memory: some of these days, when we are together, I will tell you who was the beginning, continuance, and end of all my reveries. Yes, I reckon when some of my bright anticipations have been realized, I will tell you many of the happy thoughts which, come what might, kept me always in good spirits.

I have almost reached my limit & have not begun to answer your questions. Say to Mrs. Hawk that I have heard nothing from Lt. Newman since I left Johnson's Island. I suppose though he has been exchanged. I heard to day that letters had been received from J. I. stating all to have gone through who were captured in 1863. This would include Lt. Randolph. I will answer your letter fully *very* soon. Love to all. God bless you my precious one.

Your devoted Wash

---

11. A reference to the Roman poet, Horace, who wrote, "Oak and brass of triple fold / Encompass'd sure that heart, which first made bold / To the raging sea to trust / A fragile bark, nor fear'd the Afric gust / With its Northern mates at strife, Nor Hyads' frown, nor South-wind fury-rife, / Mightiest power that Hadria knows, / Wills he the waves to madden or compose. See Horace, *The Odes and Carmen Saeculare of Horace*, trans. John Conington (London: George Bell and Sons, 1882). *Perseus Digital Library* (http://data.perseus.org/citations/urn:cts:latinLit:phi0893.phi001.perseus-eng1:1.3 : accessed on April 22, 2017).

Division 34 Fort Delaware April 2nd 1865

To day is Sunday, my darling, but I know you will not think the worse of me for devoting a part of it to you my own conscience acquits me of any wrong in it. I can't help keep thinking about you, you know, and where can be the harm in giving expression to thought, to convince me that I am wrong in writing to you on Sunday,[12] would prove that I do wrong to think of you on that day, and, if I know myself at all, that is a theorem which the combined wisdom & learning of the world can't drive into my brain. There is only one way to change the current of my thoughts now, and this is to dig down its banks and let the life out.

Several things in your last letter were news to me. I had not the slightest idea that Willie Meade had or was going to marry any body, and I am still totally in the dark as to whom the lady is. Rose is the only one I can fix upon at all, and surely I am out in that thought. Jennie never mentioned it to me, nor has she said a word about Cousin Nannie & Mr. Dunlap, but I shouldn't be at all surprised about the latter case. I had an idea of my own before I was captured as to what the young gentleman was after. Of course I never said anything that early in the day, for had I done so the good folks of Old Hanover would have set me down for a sacrilegious heathen. I have met Lt. Haymaker, have not been introduced to him, but got a friend to point him out to me the first day I got here. I heard he was corresponding with you, and of course wanted to see him immediately. I have met him several times in a game of ball, and have formed a very favorable opinion of him. He has a fine open face, and seems a great favorite with all his associates. I intend to cultivate his acquaintance first good chance I get. I don't need money just now; some was sent me from Baltimore a few days ago. I won't *write you*, dearest, my thanks for your kind offer of assistance, that is what I say to my friends generally. I will wait until I see you, then I will be able to convey to you some idea of the pleasure you have given me. I don't know what to tell you about the probability of my staying here long. I hope I shall remain here until exchanged, but there is the rub.[13] That is a point of time I have long since ceased to calculate, from the simple fact that heretofore every calcula-

---

12. Wash worries that writing letters might violate the Sabbath as a day of prayer and devotion.

13. "There is the rub" is an idiom used to indicate when something becomes difficult or problematic. See Shakespeare's *Hamlet*, act 3, scene 1, when the Prince of Denmark delivers his most famous soliloquy and uses the phrase.

tion founded upon reasonable & hopeful grounds has been proved false
by experience. And if I *can't* think the day near, I *won't* prophesy it to be
distant. One thing has been in my mind ever since your letter came viz:
"the verdict of all Dixie." I am at a dead loss what to say on the subject, all
because I have no idea when I will be exchanged, and, when I am to be
in Hanover too, it is to my intent, for once in my life, to side against "All
Dixie." How from my soul I do acknowledge your wish, that there was no
war in the land, and we were together *this* evening, and I will add, *every*
evening, indeed we would be happy. I have an abiding faith that God will
unite us before *very* long, and all our lives we will be the more blessed &
happy, because of the perfect trust the last 18 months have given us in
each other. Cheer up, my beloved, "God will bless us." Good bye

    Your own devoted Wash Nelson

P.S. Love to All. I received the stamps didn't have room to mention them
in my last.

No. 3[14]   "Home" April 4th 1865

I have written to you twice my dear Wash since the reception of your
note, telling of your arrival at Fort Delaware, which was two weeks ago,
and not another line have I received from you in all that time. I was again
beginning to think you must have left, when H. received a letter from
Richard Page, stating that you were still there. I am so impatient for a
letter, I hardly know what to do with myself. *Surely* you have written. I
cannot think you would allow so long a time to elapse without sending me
a line of love. It seems almost an impossibility that our correspondence
should continue uninterrupted for a little while. I suppose it is prevented
by some people, who are envious of the happiness of others[.] "Dear
knows" I think they might allow us that pleasure, we have been deprived
of enough already. But I will stop grumbling, as it won't better the state
of affairs. Perhaps the longer we are separated the better we learn to appreciate each other. I believe I have nothing new to write to you. Old Clip
is as dull as ever, and looks rather the worse for wear. The upper street is
a wreck of its former self, from houses having been burned. Many of the
houses on this street are perforated by bullets and shells, ours among

---

14. Mollie has begun to number her letters so that Wash will know whether any have
been lost en route. Later in this letter, she asks him to do likewise.

the number, however *we* have added an improvement to the place by having a new porch built. Yesterday the dull monotony of our lives was broken in upon the arrival of the news of the "fall of Petersburg["] which report we received "cum grano salis [with a grain of salt]," as we do all such. The thought of not receiving our annual visit this summer, causes many a pang of regret, but still we hope we shall not be disappointed.[15] What do you think of it? Fannie is at present giving us a dish of the paper. The campaign has opened, and battles are raging furiously.[16] I wonder which of our friends have been killed. O! me I *can't* say what I want to, so I will change the subject. Do you ever play chess now? Lizzie and I play occasionally. I am so anxious to become proficient, but I practice so little, I fear I never shall. Wash, will you please number all your letters, that I may know if any are lost. Write on the blank half sheet that I sent: it is larger than the generality of paper, and you can put more on a page. Aunt Lizzie's niece Sadie Glass is spending the Winter and spring here, and Lizzie is teaching her. She becomes quite disheartened sometimes, thinks her scholar does not learn so rapidly as she ought. Fannie has two scholars, and Harriot one, music scholar. Teaching school seems to be the fashion now a days. I haven't turned "school marm" yet. I received a letter from Lt. Haymaker yesterday, and shall send him an answer to-morrow. He is going to send me his photograph in his next. He wrote to ask for mine, but I declined sending it. By the way what has become of my picture? Have you managed to keep it, in all your travels. I still have your badge, though I have kept it through much tribulation.[17] I had a good scare about it last Winter, which I will tell you of when we meet. We will have *so* much to talk about then, alas, when will it be! I hope I have not made my letter too long. All send much love to you. If I do not hear from you soon, I *shant write to you any more*. Tell me all the Hanover news. Good night. May Heaven shield you from all spiritual and bodily injury prays your devoted

Mollie

---

15. Mollie again uses coded language to express her desire for a spring campaign to return northern Virginia to Confederate rule.

16. Mollie is referring to the spring campaign of 1865 that ended with the surrender of General Robert E. Lee's Army of Northern Virginia.

17. In 1863, as a way of reinforcing good conduct in battle, companies in the Army of Northern Virginia voted that certain men receive badges of distinction. Joseph T. Glatthaar, *General Lee's Army: From Victory to Collapse* (New York: Free Press, 2008), 326.

Division 34 Fort Delaware April 6th, 1865

I am reaping the fruit, my dearest love, of letting so long a time lapse between my first and second letter to you, aching to hear from you, yet conscious that I have no right to expect a letter for some days to come. I have already told you why I put off writing; in [the] future I intend to have the right to look for one from you almost any day, a right I will easily establish as there is but one thing gives me more pleasure than my part of our correspondence, and that is your part of it. Since receiving your two letters, I have been wondering how on earth I managed to bear so patiently eight whole months without one line from you. Your mention of a resource in old letters solves the question for me, when I remember how regularly every Sunday I used to take out all the letters I have had from you since my capture, and read over and think over every word in them: it was a great treat to me, and the impression is still fresh upon my mind, of how rapidly and pleasantly many a Sunday morning has passed by. What would I do but for you, dearest, any way? It is true that it is a sad thing to be so long absent from one so dearly loved, and that there is pain in constant ungratified longing, but to me the blank would be far more terrible, even supposing it a natural one with no shipwrecked hopes beneath it. Speaking of blighted hopes, reminds me how completely all mine of an early Exchange are played out. The evacuation of Richmond, and the consequent status of things will, I fear, make Exchange a dead letter for some time to come. Well, "Hope springs eternal in the human breast,"[18] is beautiful poetry, and the purest truth. I wish I could lay my heart bare to you, with all its hopes and fears. I am sure you would not dislike or regret anything you might see. You might perhaps gently rebuke me for doating too fondly on any mortal being, but I would understand even that, you wouldn't be in earnest you know, but only showing what should be taken for a proper amount of self-depreciations. I am rejoiced to hear that Phil and Fanny are getting on so happily. How I wish I could have made one of your party. I don't envy Phil his happiness the least in the world, but I do begrudge him the blessing which he could not appreciate, that of being with you. You spoke of what little idea either of us had, when we parted, of how long our separation would be. Do you not remember me saying, "Just suppose I should be captured now, and kept in prison until the war is over." And your answer, "you must not make such evil s[u]ppositions." It was one of the first things came into my

---

18. Alexander Pope, *An Essay on Man: Being the First Book of Ethic Epistles. To Henry St. John, L. Bolingbroke* (London: printed by John Wright, for Lawton Gilliver, 1734).

mind when I was taken. I have written to Mrs. Massie since I came back, but have not heard from her yet. I received one letter from her while at Fort Pulaski. In it she spoke of you, as she generally does, and sent her love to you. Willie Carter,[19] who is here with me, says I must always remember him to you all whenever I write. Poor fellow, he was paroled to Philadelphia two nights ago to see his dying sister.[20] Good night, my own darling. May God bless you. Do write as often as you can.

    Your devoted Wash Nelson

No. 4   "Home" April 9th 1865

Your letter, bearing date April 2nd came to hand yesterday, making two letters received from you in the last week, which have fully compensated for my previous disappointments. Your reason for not having written before is an acceptable excuse, and I wonder now that I had not forethought enough to account for your silence, but I was *so* impatient to hear I know you will excuse me. I am glad you received the package, and am only sorry that I did not make it larger, but I was doubtful about its reaching you was the reason. Your friends in Balt.[21] have been very kind. I hope you are now as comfortable as circumstances will admit. Well Wash, how did you stand the news of "the fall of Richmond"?[22] As philosophically as I did, I hope. I fear however it will have its effect upon some. The "good people of Hanover" are I suppose in the lines, and will have to become accustomed to the hardships that we have been enduring for the last three years. It has been said that this war was sent upon us to chasten us for our sins: if that is the case, we must indeed have been a wicked people, for we have been severely scourged. However, it is my opinion, that "whom the Lord loveth, He chasteneth." As soon as the mail communications are established, we hope to hear often from your home. I believe I am almost selfish enough to wish that under existing

---

19. William Carter (b. ca. 1837) lived in Clarke County, Va., before the Civil War. 1850 U.S. Census, Clarke County, Va., population schedule, District 112, p. 201A (stamped), dwelling 471, family 471, William Carter; digital image, *Ancestry.com* (http://ancestry.com : accessed April 26, 2017); citing NARA microfilm publication M324, 432, roll 940.

20. William Carter's sister, Evelyn, was nine years younger than he.

21. Baltimore, Md.

22. The "fall of Richmond" refers to the evacuation of Richmond by Confederates on April 2, 1865, and the immediate capture of the city by Union troops. James McPherson, *Battle Cry of Freedom: The Civil War Era* (Oxford, England: Oxford University Press, 1988), 846–47.

circumstances you will not be exchanged, because we are now entirely cut off from all communication with our friends in the South that writing will be our only pleasure, however, I know you are anxious to bear a part of the coming struggles, and I hope I am patriot enough to make the sacrifice. Is the exchange still going on? I fear late events will put a stop to it. Willie Mead married, or was to marry on the 17th of March—Miss Nannie Winston of Orange Co. I suppose, from all accounts, he and Church had to leave their brides behind and *run* for their lives. I don't suppose they could be encumbered with *such unnecessary luggage.* I hope they managed to make good time so as not to be captured. I am glad you like Lt. Haymaker's looks, and I hope you may not be disappointed when you make his acquaintance. He passed through this place on his way North, and obtained permission to stop here a few minutes. Then it was, that we made our arrangements to correspond. He sent me a beautiful ring and seems very grateful for my attention. Mary Myers[23] has a correspondent at Fort Del. Lt. Ransom whom she has instructed to make your acquaintance. I do not know him personally, but expect he is a nice young fellow.

I have been in great distress for the last few days. Some villain poisoned my newfoundland dog, and he suffered so terribly that I had to have him shot. I have been almost tempted to apply to myself the quotation, "O! ever thus from Childhoods hour."[24] I have spent the last week pretty much in the grave yard fixing up the soldiers graves. I wish you could see them. Harriot was at Sister Anne's yesterday. She desired her love to you. Her oldest son is 18, but I fear he intends to disgrace his name by avoiding the service. I hope I am mistaken. I should be grieved to see anyone, bearing my father's name, act in such a cowardly manner.

What day of the month will be your birth day? It comes in April I think.[25] This will be the 2nd you have passed in prison. Your season of trail has been a tedious one, trust you will come out purified by affliction. Trials have been well compared to the "winds employed to fill our sails

---

23. Mary E. Myers, born about 1837 and daughter of John Myers and older sister of John W. Myres (see chap. 3), lived in Middleway, Jefferson County, Va., in 1860. She was a teacher. 1860 U.S. Census, Jefferson County, W.Va., population schedule, p. 906 (stamped), dwelling 395, family 380, John G. and Mary E. Myers, *Ancestry.com* (http://ancestry.com : accessed April 25, 2017); citing NARA microfilm publication M324, 653, roll 1355.

24. Thomas Moore, *Lalla Rookh: An Oriental Romance* (London: Printed for Longman, Hurst, Rees, Orme, and Brown, by A. Strahan, 1817), 188.

25. Wash's birthday was actually May 27, 1840.

and bring us home to the harbor of ever lasting peace."[26] All send love. Affectionately yours Mollie

6   Division 34 Fort Delaware April 12th 1865

It is not a happy time with me at present, as you may well believe, my love, and oh! with what delight I look at the one bright place in my heart, which even in this sad time consoles me beyond all description. You, my darling, have for the last few days been more in my thoughts than ever. And though made happier the more I think, from the conviction of possessing your constant love, yet I must confess to some very anxious thoughts about you now. How could it be otherwise. Believing as I do that your happiness & mine are identical when I can form no idea what will be my future fate—and how it will affect you. I can lay my hand on my chest and say that for myself alone I fear nothing, I have endeavored to follow in the path of duty, with all my might, and be the consequences what they may I have & can have no regrets. But you, my beloved, you may be made unhappy through me, this is what makes me anxious. I would rather die than resign your love, and yet in proportion to my love, is my anxiety about your happiness. I think I could banish all care, if I could be sure of your affection, and at the same time certain that no evil which might come to me would affect you. How I am talking as if I *expected* & was preparing you for some great calamity. When the truth is I only know the *possibility* of such a thing. I didn't intend to write you this sort of a letter, but somehow my heart will turn its truthful side to you. Were I sure no eyes but your own would see it I wouldn't even care how open it lay. You could not find much fault with what is all your own. In my answer to your last letter I said nothing about my Home for the reason that I have not heard a word from them since I came back here. I very much doubt whether they know where I am. I have not written to them yet. I suppose that after a little[,] letters will go straight through Richmond. Who would have thought it? If we could be disinterested spectators of our own lives, the ups & downs and unexpected turns would be very amusing.

---

26. John R. Macduff, *The Hart and the Water-Brooks; A Practical Exposition of the Forty-Second Psalm* (New York: Robert Carter and Brothers, 1860), 189. Mollie misquotes Macduff, who writes, "Trials have been well compared to the winds God employs to fill our sails and fetch us home to the harbor of everlasting peace!" The slight error suggests that she quoted from memory.

How knocked to pieces your little town must be. Carter Berkely gave me an account of the fight there.[27] Where were you, Mollie, when bullets were flying through your house and the porch blown up? You are quite a veteran; this is not the first time, if I remember rightly, that you have seen & heard something besides the "*pomp* and *circumstances* of War." I read a letter to day from Harriot, through which I learned the death of your Newfoundland dog. I remember mighty well seeing him on guard the night you & I returned from your sister Annie's and went out to see that some little chickens were comfortably & safely housed. I envied the dog that night because he had a place in the heart which had been denied me. I would have given worlds then to have elicited as tender a word, and received as affectionate a pat on the head as he did. Well "requiescat in pace." I don't envy him, or any one now. I have faith to believe that the occasion would bring me the blessing. Tell me, is my belief well founded? I know it is, but it is so sweet to see your assertion of it. Best love to all. Don't let's count letters[28] with each other. Write whenever you can. I will do the same.

God bless you and make you always happy, my darling, earnestly prays your devoted

Wash Nelson

7   Division 34. Fort Delaware April 15th 1865

I received your letter yesterday evening, my darling Mollie; the violets are mighty sweet, and as I read your dear letter, there steals over me along with the soft perfume of the flowers a glad sense of happiness at the love & trust you repose in me. You are very right in your belief that I will excuse what you term *your want of fore thought.* Did all your wants bring such comfort to my heart as your excuse of that one, it is to be feared I would wish you to be very needy. I think the best conclusion we both can come to, is that we need no excuse in each other's eyes. And that hereafter we will only use them to exemplify their uselessness. I will tell you one thing that astonishes me, and that is how I managed to put off answering your letter until this morning. What do you think of my reading a novel when I should have been writing to you? I won't attempt to justify myself, for I feel that I need never, I am perfectly sure that I had rather have a

---

27. Battle of Smithfield Crossing, August 26–29, 1864.

28. "Do not let us count." In other words, Wash is telling Mollie not to worry about how often or how much they write, given the current circumstances.

few words with you than read the best novel ever written, and I believe you know it. I ask you the question because I want your help to explain a thing that really puzzles me. I had a letter yesterday from Mrs. Massie written to me at Fort Pulaski. It was in answer to one in which I had told her that I never got letters from any one and she asks me if I am not getting uneasy about Miss M. I have kept all her letters for the express purposes of showing them to you. And mighty kind letters they are. She has been as good as a mother to me since I have been in prison. My birthday doesn't come in April at all. It will be the 27th of May. My last was spent in the Hospital at Point Lookout. I passed the day thinking of you, and yes I will confess it, in writing *poetry* or *rhyme* or whatever it may be called. How the coming one will be spent remains to be seen. I hope I won't spend many more in my present fix, or I will be so old looking you will never recognize me. What you call my trials I have never considered so intolerable. I was never yet in a bad fix, but what some one with me was worse off, hence there was always cause for thankfulness. You have yourself to thank that I can't make a virtue of my trials. You who have been under all circumstances an unfailing source of happiness to me.

I had heard of the death of your dog before your letter came. I sympathize with you, dearest, in all your sorrows. O! if I could be with you to help you bear them. I *can't* tell you what I think about Richmond. Judge me in all things by your knowledge of me. My compliments to miss Mary Myers, say to her, her friend has not as yet obeyed instructions. Do you see much of your sister Anne now? Have you forgotten my commission to you to make her like me? You know how much I was taken with her, give her my love. Can you tell me anything of the Long-Branch family? And how does poor Mrs Randolph bear the loss of her two sons. Rob was at home the day Tom & I were captured, and we were thinking all along what a lucky fellow he was not to have shared our fate.

I never heard of the Miss Winston Willie Meade married before, those having their young brides now, will I fear have to bid them long farewell. You term them "*useless luggage.*"[29] I agree with you if you leave out the adjective. Because "*Riches* are the baggage of *virtue.*" Had you said *indispensable*, we should have agreed exactly. I know that is what you meant. Love to all. Good bye. God bless you, my own love, your ever devoted,

   Wash

---

29. A famous maxim of Francis Bacon. See, for example, *The Physical and Metaphysical Works of Lord Bacon, Including the Advancement of Learning and Novum Organum*, ed. Josheph Devey (London: George Bell and Sons, 1808), 259.

No. 5   Saturday April 15th 1865

My Dear Wash—This is a terribly gloomy day, and as the weather, independent of outward circumstances, always affect my spirits, I am feeling
pretty "blue," but as I protest against sending a prisoner any but cheerful
letters, I must try and shake off all care. It is hard enough for us to bear
this heavy trial, then what must be the feeling of the prisoners, situated
as they are. I wish you would write me what you think of the present state
of affairs. It is to me a mystery that I cannot solve.

Our wise-acre's[30] say the War is over, and many I believe are glad to
have peace at any terms. It almost drives me wild, when I think of the
many loved ones, who have given up their lives, that we might be free,
and can it be, that they have died in vain. O! no! Surely a just God in
Heaven will in the end bring it all out right. We have been looking forward to the arrival at home of some of the paroled soldiers, but have
been disappointed so far. It is very strange they do not come, if we have
heard the proper statement. What is to become of the prisoners? Do you
think they will be paroled, or are we to bear still longer this cruel separation, added to our other trials. I suppose you have seen an account of
Evelyn Carter's death.[31] She went to Philadelphia, hoping the trip would
be beneficial to her delicate health, and there died. I have not heard
from you at all this week, am expecting a letter hourly. Lizzie recd a letter
from Capt. Pointer, written in a very desponding strain. You must try and
cheer him up. Keep a brave heart yourself, and comfort those around
you. It is my firm belief that "there's a better time coming." My faith is
strong on the justice of our cause, but if we fail, we must bear up cheerfully. H is spending the day at Aunt Betsey's. We feel very lonely since
they left. You would feel amused to see Fannie and Aunt Betsey cooking,
&c. They have no servant, except a little girl. I am going up this evening
to milk the cow, as neither of them know how. We will make a great deal
of fun over our misfortunes. Ma and Aunt Fannie both send love to you.

Write often to your devotedly attached

  M—

---

30. A somewhat scornful or contemptuous appellation for foolish individuals who wish
to appear wise. Mollie does not seem to convey the scorn in the original meaning.

31. The younger sister of Wash and Mollie's friend Willie Carter.

CHAPTER 5

Spring to Autumn 1865

Surrender and Allegiance

By the close of April 1865, the war had ended and Wash faced pledging an oath of allegiance to the United States. He and Mollie waited anxiously for his release from prison and return home, a homecoming that did not occur until June. Thereafter, correspondence between Wash and Mollie no longer left each other's hands unsealed so that the eyes of a prison inspector could read them. No longer confined to a single-page restriction, Wash wrote about his thoughts and emotions even more than usual, turning his attention to marriage and the coming wedding Mollie was planning. Although playful, these postwar letters reveal a degree of nervousness about their future lives together as husband and wife, particularly in terms of gender roles in marriage. They also reveal the couple's anxiety about the South's new social order during Reconstruction. For Wash and Mollie, as was true of so many former Confederates, the relations between state and nation, northerners and southerners, men and women, whites and blacks were uncertain and unstable, leading to types of violence that were quite different from those of war and imprisonment.

---

6   Sunday morning Apr. 23rd 1865

My dear Wash,

Although there is preaching in town today, something we have not had for some time, I have remained at home to have a pleasant chat with my *poor prisoner*. The Methodist minister from Charleston came up yesterday to hold service for our citizens. The Episcopal brethren of the surrounding country never take compassion upon the poor *deluded Clippers* as you may suppose, when I tell you, the last time I heard a sermon in my own church, was the day cousin Bob preached for us, after our return from Hanover. Perhaps you remember. For the last two days I have been busy, preparing a box of eatables for you and cousin Richard, and now it is nicely packed, and ready to be sent off tomorrow morning. It is not as large a box as we would like to have sent, but we thought perhaps the small size might insure its safe delivery.

The tobacco and jelly-cake sister Annie sends you with her love. Yesterday, when we were packing the box, some one suggested that we should leave out the tobacco, and give place for something else, but I put my veto upon it, knowing your partiality for the article. And now that I have told about the box, I will proceed to answer your letter. Your last—no 6—I did not exactly understand. Surely you do not think that because of late events, my feelings towards you should change. I cannot think less of a brave soldier, because he has been overpowered by numbers. We have acted as we believed to be right, we were inspired by the noble principles of duty, then why should we feel humiliated? Though we may have ceased to strike for success, and bright hopes for the future have ceased to animate us, still it is very comforting to have approval of a quiet conscience, and to feel that we have always followed in the path of duty. Cheer up then, and do not for one moment feel that you are disgraced by what has happened. Nearly all the soldiers from this place and vicinity have returned. It looks quite like old times to see them, and the young ladies have ceased to lament the want of beaux.

Lem Dandridge dined here yesterday on his way home. The other two arrived some days ago. He inquired very particularly after you, and sent his love. He says that cousin Wm N. "dies harder than any one he has seen yet," but the old Gen[l] he thinks, is right glad to get home again. He also told us that cousin Randolph was to be married to a miss Grattan[1] from Richmond. Dudley has gotten home, and we are hoping he will come in soon to see us. I think he can give us some tidings of our friends in Hanover. Did I in my last letter lead you to infer that our porch was blown up by a shell? If so, I must undeceive you. A shell *did* burst at the steps, when we were all at the door, but no damage was done, except to

---

1. Lizzie G. Grattan (1837–1921) was the second eldest child of Peachy Ridgeway Grattan, a lawyer, and Jane E. Grattan. She was twenty-two years old in 1860 and took charge of a school for girls in Richmond in 1869. She never married. 1860 U.S. Census, Henrico County, Va., population schedule, Richmond Ward 2, p. 152, dwelling 775, family 921, Lizzie G. Grattan; digital image, *Ancestry.com* (http://ancestry.com : accessed April 23, 2017); citing NARA microfilm publication M324, 653, roll 1352. Also see Virginius Dabney, *Richmond: The Story of a City*, rev. ed. (1976; repr., Charlottesville, Va.: University of Virginia Press, 1990), 231.

the windows, which were shivered. Wash, Sister Annie requested me to send you the enclosed dollar, and ask you to buy her a Fort ring. I have rec^d Lt. H. photograph, and think him quite a fine looking fellow. It is well taken. Can't you send me yours? All send love. Remember us all to our cousins at Ft. Delaware. I hope you will enjoy the contents of the box. Mizpah[2]—Ever yours

    M—

7   Smithfield April 28th 1865

I wrote on Sunday my Dear Wash, telling you that I would forward the next day a box of eatables for yourself and cousin Richard, and just when I was feeling so confident that it was rapidly approaching Fort Delaware, received a note saying the agent at Kearneysville[3] had refused to take it, upon the plea that prisoners are not allowed to receive boxes. I cannot express my disappointment. I was so anxious that you should receive it. There were two other boxes sent from here at the same time, in one of which I sent some things to Lt. H.,[4] but they were all still at the depot, and will have to remain there until we can procure some conveyance to get them home. We should not have prepared the boxes had we not received assurances from many sources that they would go with perfect safety, and it is very provoking to feel that our labour was all for naught, but I, for one, have been schooled to bear disappointment since this War. Such is your case also n'est-ce pas [is it not]? Your last letter was nearly two weeks old when it reached me. How did that happen? They generally come in five or six days from the time they are written. I am very glad you have kept Mrs. Massie's letters. I shall enjoy reading them some day. I have seen a great deal of Sister Annie this spring. Don't know that I have taken any great pains to make her like you, but think I can truthfully say, you possess a large share of her warm heart. She always sends best love to you. Cousin Hugh Pendleton and Coz. Julia were here yesterday. Harriot and I intend walking to Thomson's tomorrow to spend the day, in the evening, the boys are to come over for us and escort us to Westwood where we will spend a few days, and then they will come home with us, and we

---

2. The Hebrew word for "watchtower." In Genesis, Laban and Jacob form a covenant on Galeed by a pillar, or watchtower: "The Lord watch between you and me, when we are absent from one another" (Genesis 31:49).

3. Kearneysville, W.Va., is located in the eastern part of the state's panhandle and is very close to what is now northern Virginia.

4. Lieutenant Haymaker.

shall keep them here as long as we possibly can. It is a great treat to us to
see our soldiers again, even under the circumstances. Mr. Francis is here,
just the same only a little more *frisky*, if possible. Fannie has gone to the
country with him to spend the day with his lady love, Miss Lizzie Fry.[5] I
believe he does not now deny his engagement, and madame Rumor says
they are to be married very soon. Lizzie is a sweet, lovely girl, and desir-
ing of a better husband than he will make, however, I suppose we must
"judge not." Do you really begin to look old or were you only jesting? I
am quite concerned, for I don't *like* old looking young people, and if you
don't put on your young handsome looks before you come to see me
I'll—What?—Nothing. I am slightly besprinkled myself, but it is a great
consolation to know that sorrow as well as age sometimes leaves its mark.
I hear that the prisoners at Pt. Lookout are to be paroled and released,
and suppose the same terms will be granted to those at Ft. Del[r]. It seems
so useless and cruel to keep them confined this lovely weather. One of
the paroled soldiers from this place was a prisoner at Elmira for some
time, and I am doubly interested in his account of prison life, though I
expected he had comparatively an easy time of it.[6] We heard from Long
Branch not long ago. They were all well and getting along finely. Lt.
R. was at Johnson's Island when last heard from. Willie Meade is at his
father-in-law's. The other boys are at home. Give our love to cousin Richard, and tell him of our good intentions "mais l'homme propose, mais
dieu dispose."[7] Mamma, Aunt Fannie and Harriot send love to you and
our other cousins.

Good bye. That God may grant us a happy meeting, and that speedily
is my earnest prayer. Devotedly yours
    Mollie

---

5. Elizabeth A. Fry (b. ca. 1838), daughter of a "day labourer," lived in nearby Frederick
County, Va. 1860 U.S. Census, Frederick County, Virginia, District 7, population schedule,
Mountain Falls, p. 672, dwelling 359, family 365, Elizabeth A. Fry; digital image, *Ancestry
.com* (http://ancestry.com : accessed April 23, 2017); citing NARA microfilm publication
M324, 653, roll 1347.

6. Elmira, N.Y., was the location of a prison camp for Confederate enlisted men. In
contrast to Mollie's expectation, enlisted men were much more crowded than officers in
northern and southern prisons. A greater proportion of Confederate prisoners died at Elmira than anywhere else in the North. Officers, however, perhaps because they were better
educated and connected than enlisted men, wrote more letters and garnered a greater
share of sympathy from people like Mollie. See Paul J. Springer and Glenn Robins, *Transforming Civil War Prisons: Lincoln, Lieber, and the Politics of Captivity* (New York: Routledge,
2015), 52; Michael P. Gray, *The Business of Captivity: Elmira and Its Civil War Prison* (Kent:
Kent State University Press, 2001), 153; James M. Gillespie, *Andersonvilles of the North: The
Myths and Realities of Northern Treatment of Civil War Confederate Prisoners* (Denton: University
of North Texas, 2008), 161.

7. The French translates loosely as "Man proposes, God disposes."

Division 38 Fort Delaware May 3rd 1865

My darling Mollie

I intended writing to you this morning, but there was quite a levee at my "bunk," so I couldn't get a chance. Richard Page and I have been anxiously attending "Box Call" for the last two days, but so far have seen no sign of *the box*. I told you in my last letter what would probably be its fate, so I won't repeat.[8]

The events of the last few days have worked a great change among the officers confined here. The surrender of Johnston's army,[9] together with the voluntary surrender of one or two members of President Davis' Cabinet have combined to force upon us the conclusion that the Southern Confederacy is indeed a thing of the past. I need not tell you how I in common with others from our dear Old State struggled against this conviction, hoped against hope, it is sufficient to say that I don't believe there is a man in the prison who has a reasonable belief that the Confederacy now exists. We have had meetings of the representatives of different states in here, and the most solemn, most affecting meeting at which I was ever present was that of the Virginia delegation the day before yesterday. The state of things was discussed from every point of view, opinions were fully & freely interchanged, and the conclusion arrived at that our government no longer existed in fact that therefore our obligations to it were at an end, and our honor could in no way be compromised by any course we might pursue with regard to it. Then came up the question, "what is our duty under the circumstances?" and the opinion was almost unanimous that we ought to return to our homes and to our loved ones, to support and to comfort them under this state of things on the following day our names were called for the third time to know whether we were willing to take the oath of Allegiance to the United States, the result was that out of 2300 officers only 161 said "No." I myself am with the majority. I acted with the approval of both my reason and my conscience as well as with the advice of my friends and brother officers. God alone knows the struggle I have had with my pride, but I have overcome it, and I feel that I have done what was right. And now, beloved, may I look to you, whom I love a thousand times better than all else in this world, for a

---

8. This letter must be missing from the collection or it did not arrive.

9. As the war came to a close, General Joseph E. Johnston (1807–91) commanded the remaining Confederate troops in the Carolinas and surrendered to William T. Sherman on April 26, 1865. John L. Bell Jr. and Brendan Wolfe, "Joseph E. Johnston (1807–1891)," *Encyclopedia Virginia*, Virginia Foundation for the Humanities, Oct. 21, 2014, http://www.EncyclopediaVirginia.org/Johnston_Joseph_E_1807-1891.

little comfort, for the cheering word that you will sustain me in the path of duty & conscience? Ah! My darling, if you only knew the rack I have been upon from the fear that by a false step now I might lose you forever, you would have some idea of how I love you. God bless you always. If you love me write immediately. Love to all.

   Your devoted Wash

Tell Ned Dandridge[10] to write to Lt. Louis Booker

Division 38 Fort Delaware May 4th 1865

Your last letter, my darling Mollie, was received just after I had mailed my last to you, so I thought it best to wait until this morning to answer it. Dick & I had been looking out anxiously for the box, though we had little expectation of getting it, and it is rather a relief to know that it did not get entirely out of your reach. Had it come here neither you nor we would have seen it any more. Any way we have the good will that sent it, and that is a great comfort to us just now. Dick tells me that he wrote to H.[11] yesterday, so you and she will get letters explaining our position at the same time. Of course, dearest, I could not say all I would have liked to say, could not, under circumstances where others would see them, urge motives which should be known to you & me alone, and plead my cause in that way which my own heart dictated and which would perhaps have given you a better idea of the pressure under which I acted than all the facts & arguments I might advance. One thing I will state on this subject now, and then I will leave it until I hear from my last to you. We have the fullest assurance that not one single Confederate officer will be paroled from Prison; this comes from high authority in Washington. I know the report you heard with regard to the Point Lookout officers to be untrue, because those officers have been *here* for nearly a week, and are in our fix exactly. You are right, my love, in saying that we have been schooled to bear disappointment; there is only one hope in my life with regard to which I can not for a moment bear the idea of disappointment. And when sometimes my reason tells me I ought to take into account all the uncertainty of this mortal life, and ought to be prepared at least to *endure* disappointment even in this hope, my heart boiling with indignant love

---

10. Possibly a relation of Lem Dandridge, whom Mollie mentioned earlier.
11. Harriot Lowndes Scollay, Mollie's sister.

says, "no," if it must come let it come and kill me all at once, to think of it is a "living death." I really don't know whether I am old looking or not, I have not looked in the glass for so long. I was speaking of my feelings rather than my appearance, but however the case may be, I know that I shall be very young looking when we meet if there is any truth in the saying "happiness makes one look young." What Cousin Randolph is it, that is to marry one of the Miss Grattan's? It can't be Ranny Page, because he has one wife already. Give my best love to your sister Anne. I hope she will get the ring I sent her. Mr Francis has turned up again has he! Does Fannie teaze [*sic*] him much, or is she charitable? Love to all. God bless you.

Your devoted Wash

12 Division 38 Fort Delaware May 10th 1865

Still at Fort Delaware, my darling, and no sign of being away from it soon that I can see; and oh! how long and how tiresome the days are getting! I thought I had patience to stand almost anything, but I find the continual expectation and the never coming reality of release almost too much for me. I look across the river, see the green fields, and sometimes fancy I hear the breeze rustling through the trees, or snuff the peach and cherry blossoms from the distance, but instead of being soothed by the gentle influence of so much beauty, I chafe like a caged tiger for freedom to roam at will. I have gained one thing by it however—a problem to solve—viz. how is it that beauty should excite passion in the heart? Not the tender passions of course that can be testified to by a world of generations and could therefore be easily accounted for. I have managed to pass a good deal of time thinking on the subject & have formed several theories. The most plausible of which is temporary insanity. Of course I don't relish this last conclusion, because vanity does not like to admit madness however slight or of however short durations, least of all do I like to admit it to you, but then logic is logic, and if correct reasoning upon my own experience brings me to an unwelcome conclusion, truth & candor require me to admit it. Besides if by my reasoning I can establish that I am not made for want of brain, flattered vanity will be fully compensated for the admission. I expect you will ask me if I am in earnest, about this—as if an "old looking young man" ever joked about anything, much less about his own failing & deficiencies. Let me comfort you by telling you that if there is any truth in it all, you are the cause of it all. If I am mad, it is for love of you; if the few remaining hairs of my

head are silvered over, and the wrinkles in my forehead too numerous to count, it is all for love of you. Why the madness, the premature age, ought to be witness to the constancy and intensity of the passion you have inspired. And am I not right to conclude that with such witnesses as these my cause cannot fail to be gained? Do you understand this letter, dearest? My space is so limited I have to write in riddles. Apply the key of your heart to all I say and you will understand me, for the plain English of it all is—I love you with an intensity that I almost tremble at, and long to see you with an agony of impatience, and I believe O sweet comforter, that you love me. Love to all. May God bless you. Write often to
    your loving, devoted Wash

Tell Lizzie he[r] fri[e]nd Capt. Points expects to leave here tomorrow.

14   Division 38 Fort Delaware May 14th 1865

You are a sweet comforter, my own Mollie, and have made me very happy by your last letter, assuring me not only of your acquiescence in what I had done,[12] but of your hearty approval the one great question with me now, is when will I be free to come to you. I imagine the opinion prevails with most of you that all we have to do now is to take the oath and then go where we please—such seems to me the most reasonable, certainly the most pleasant manner of procedure, but I suppose we are such important personages that we cannot be disposed of with so little form. And I suppose one might as well look for an off hand decision in "Chancery" as a speedy deliverance here.[13] So you better not expect me very soon or I fear I will *have* to disappoint you. Although you are exactly right in taking it for granted I will come via "Clip," you must remember that I am not master of my own actions, therefore if I am a long time getting to you, the delay will be against my will & against all my efforts. Two things may happen—we may be here for a good while yet, and also when sent from here we Virginians may be all shipped to Richmond in a lump. in the latter case I must of course go home first, but whatever happens the

---

12. Mollie must have responded to Wash's letters, assuring him that taking the Oath of Allegiance did not besmirch his character, though there is no record of her reply other than this letter from Wash.

13. Wash seems to be using an arcane legal metaphor of chancery law to underscore how slowly his release will occur.

Valley[14] is the point on which my eye is fixed, and the *gem* of the Valley the object I am striving to reach, I have seen its beauty, I have proved its genuineness and know its value, it is the one treasure in which my whole heart is absorbed, and to win & to wear it is the aim of my existence. You need not have hesitated, dearest, to advise me. I am of course flattered & pleased by your confidence in my judgment, but it would surprise me if your advice and my judgment did not point to the same conclusion in almost every question. I told "Cousin Richard" about the room awaiting him & myself. He is very anxious to see you all, but at present seems to think he must go to Lynchburg as soon as possible, but aided, as I know I am, by his wishes I hope to convert him yet. I am sorry you did not get the letter with cousin Annie's ring—it is just my luck though, and does not much surprise me, it was quite a pretty ring, the design, a vine with a dove in the centre, was very nearly done and I wanted to get it so much there are not many pretty rings for sale here now, but the first pretty one I come upon I will get, and keep until I see her. I have received *all* your letters so far, the last one you forgot to number. I had not heard a word of Ranny Page's Wife's death. And he is about to marry again! Well, I expect I will hear of many strange things that have happened since that day away back yonder when I was captured; my status by the time I get back from here will approximate to that of the old fellow who took a 20 years nap.[15] But love to all. God bless you my darling.

Your devoted Wash

Sunday evening 21st May 1865

My dear Wash

I intended writing to you this morning, but after performing my usual Sunday morning's duties, felt so sleepy that I was compelled to take a nap, and when I awoke, dinner was ready, so that I could not accomplish this pleasant duty before evening. Imagine if you please a little figure, dressed in a light calico dress and pink ribands, hair put up plainly in a net, countenance rather sad than otherwise, seated in one corner of the parlor, with no one near to disturb the current of her thoughts, writing to an absent loved one, and you have the personification of your honorable

14. The Shenandoah Valley.

15. An allusion to Washington Irving's famed "Rip Van Winkle," first published in serial form in *The Sketch Book of Geoffey Crayon, Gent, No. 1* (New York: C. S. Van Winkle, 1819).

servant. Three letters from you last week made me almost happy, particularly those in which you mention your intention to return home this way. I shall be more impatient now than before, because I had given up all hope of seeing you before your visit to Hanover. It is not possible that you would like to "see me right well,["] is it? Really it is very strange that after nearly two years absence, you should have any desire of the kind. It seems to me you ought to wish rather to see your friends at home, than one, who has been to you the cause of so much suffering. Lt. H. got out through the influence of his uncle. Think you not that your friends in New York or Balt. could do something for you. I think they can if you will write to them on the subject. Yesterday we all spent the day at Mrs Beall's, sewing for her son, who has returned, with no clothes such as he would be allowed to wear. I brought a shirt home with me to make this week, and of course I shall take great pleasure in sewing on it. Fannie is in Loudoun,[16] paying a visit to Mr Francis' family. Poor child! The trip will recall many sad reminiscences but still she seemed very anxious to go. She expects to bring one of the young ladies home with her, when she returns which I suppose will not be in less than a week, as the last rains will no doubt cause the river to rise.

It is supposed that Miss Francis is coming on to attend her brother's wedding, though I don't pretend to know any thing about it. If Fan does, she keeps it very closely, you know she is a pretty good hand at keeping a secret. The flowers are looking beautifully now. I know a sight of them would be refreshing to you. Lt. H. made a parlor of the garden when he was here. I hope you will be here to help us enjoy the strawberries. They will be in perfection about the 1st June, and I hope you will make it convenient to leave Ft. Del. by that time. I must confess that I was disappointed at not receiving a long letter by the Lt. I am so tired of these one page letters. It would have been safe with him I think. He delivered your *"respects."* I have forgotten to number my letters lately and now I don't know what number this one ought to have. You must continue to number yours however. I suggested the plan, and have failed to perform my part. It has been raining, raining, raining all day long, and still it rains. It seems as though the clouds were weeping themselves away over the depravity of man. Rec^d a note from Sister Annie. She sends love to you, and says you must take the oath, and come home. She expects to go

---

16. Loudon County is in northern Virginia.

to Balt. next week. Kinloch Nelson[17] is engaged to Fenton McGuire.[18] She had to take him at last to get rid of him. My space is out. Good bye. Write to me often.

    Mollie

17   Division 38 Fort Delaware May 27th 1865

I awake this morning dearest Mollie, to the fact that I to day enter upon the second quarter century of my existence a little over 1/15th of which I have passed in prison. My last birthday I spent at Point Lookout, thinking of you and wondering what the coming 12 months had in store of us; to day I am occupied pretty much in the same way, with the difference that while thinking of you I am writing to instead of about you. It is a miserable day. Cold and rainy, and I would be right down blue but for the pleasant thoughts and bright hopes about you which fill my heart with a joy too great to be driven away from any sort of weather. Your letter received and answered yesterday, and which I have just read over again speaks mighty sweetly to me this morning. I would not have missed getting it yesterday evening for something pretty it comforts me so much and that you managed so that it reached me just at this time adds another to the countless links "which bind me to thee." Do you feel very solemnly on your birthdays? I do to day. Many little pleasantries suggest themselves to me, but I don't write any of them because they do not come from my heart. I think I begin to feel the truth and power of the line "Life is real, life is earnest,"[19] and with this feeling comes the belief that the recognition of the fact and a course of life based upon it is the true way to meet the ends of the Almighty in our creation, and the only way to secure real and lasting happiness. The great difficulty is to act upon this

17. Rev. Kinloch Nelson (b. 1839) of Clarke County, Va., was youngest of eight children of Thomas and Mildred Nelson. He attended the University of Virginia and joined the Eta Chapter of Delta Kappa Epsilon fraternity in 1860. This was also the fraternity to which George Washington Nelson belonged. Afterward, Kinloch studied divinity and was ordained a priest at Episcopal Theological Seminary (now Virginia Theological Seminary). He later taught at the same institution. See A. N. Brockway, ed., *Catalogue of the Delta Kappa Epsilon Fraternity* (New York: Council Publishing Company, 1900), 179.

18. Grace Fenton McGuire (1838–1904) was the daughter of John P. McGuire of Essex County, Va. She and Kinloch Nelson married in 1868. Richard Channing Moore Page, *Genealogy of the Page Family in Virginia. Also a Condensed Account of the Nelson, Walker, Pendelton and Randolph Families* (New York: Press of the Publishers' Printing Co., 1893), 184.

19. Henry Wadsworth Longfellow, "A Psalm of Life," *Knickerbocker Magazine* (October 1838).

belief, the beauties of "myth" and the poetry of the "ideal" take such fast hold upon us, that we forget that the life they treat of is only compara-tive, and thus forgetting [we] lose the benefit of the lesson they teach. O! how I wish I could have a good long talk with you to day my darling. I feel a solemn joy as I gaze down the stream of time, the objects of my gaze fade from view in the obscurity of the future, but there is no fear for their fate, the shadow that hides them is simply "the unknown." Fear & doubt have nothing to do with it. And the solemn joy still remains wild & yet restrained in its intensity. I want to talk to you about all this, I want your thoughts, your fears and hopes about the future. Yes, love, I want to measure all your strength & all your weakness. I want each because I love each as part of yourself, and I want both, because I love them beyond expression as constituting yourself. Good bye beloved, your own devoted
    Wash

Love to all

Smithfield May 27th 1865

I wrote you on Sunday last my dear Wash, but owing to the destruction of the bridge at the Ferry,[20] suppose you did not receive my letter as soon as you would have done under other circumstances. Owing to this catastro-phe, we have received no mail this week until to day, and as you may imag-ine I was sadly disappointed that there was no letter for me, after waiting so long, I surely hoped to be rewarded for my patience but still I have not despaired for this week, as we have sent a special messenger down for todays mail. Aunt Fannie received a letter this morning from Capt Halsey, of whose captivity we were not aware until a short time ago. She recom-mended you to his acquaintance I believe, but he mentioned that he al-ready knew you. I got a letter not long ago from an officer at Ft. Del., whom I met only once during the first year of the war, and have not seen since. I shall not answer the letter, as I do not care to enter into correspondence with any more strangers. I feel deeply for our poor prisoners, and think that we ought to do every thing in our power to alleviate their suffering although my friend seems to think they have no one to care for them now.
    How pleasantly and quickly a rainy day passes off, when one has an interesting book to read. Yesterday I scarcely noticed the weather, being

---

20. Harpers Ferry, W.Va.

completely absorbed in "The Hidden Path," one of Marion Harland's works.[21] I admire her style so much. Do you not? I received just now from Maj. Beall a sweet little note of thanks for making a shirt for him. It is my first attempt, and I am quite found of my success. You see I am *learning in time.* I believe I tell you Wash of almost every little incident that occurs, but nevertheless I flatter myself that nothing that concerns your humble servant will be uninteresting to you. N'est se pas? [Isn't it so?]

Our neighborhood has been very gay lately—dancing parties and pic nics in abundance, given to the returned soldier's. There is to be a large pic-nic next week on the Opequon,[22] to which I am invited, but shall decline going, as I rarely attend such places. People now, seem to have lost all interest in the country, and think of nothing but fashion and dress. O! I had almost forgotten to tell the *joyful news.* Aunt Fannie has actually got a *beau*!!! He is the nicest old widower you ever saw, and we are all crazy for the *match.* You would be amused to see how gallant the old fellow is. Came down in all the rain, and escorted her up street to sing for him. Thinks she has an *angelic voice.* Of course we nearly tease the life out of her, though she takes it very well. Fannie is still in Loudoun. We somewhat expected her home to day, but I reckon they will not be able to cross the river yet-a-while.

And so you have been compelled to pass another birth day in prison. Well! How did you celebrate it? I thought much of you all day, and wished O! how ardently that we could spend it together. You have now been a prisoner nineteen months, and I little know I reckon what sufferings you have endured, but never mind when you come home, we will forget the past in the enjoyment of the present. I often sit down, and imagine how I will feel when you come, and my heart bounds at every footstep after night. I have several times gone to the door, almost hoping to meet you. Mamma and all send love to you and cousin Richard. Harriot is talking of paying a visit to Clarksburg[23] this summer, but I want her to wait until things are more settled. Good bye. May God bless you and soon restore to you home and loved ones. Devotedly and tenderly your

Mollie

---

21. Marion Harland is the nom de plume of Mary Virginia Terhune, a well-known author who spent most of her life in New Jersey. *The Hidden Path* (London: G. Routledge Co., 1855) was her second novel.

22. A tributary of the Potomac River, which flows through Winchester, Va., into West Virginia.

23. Clarksburg, W.Va., located in Harrison County, in the north-central part of the state.

Saturday morning June 3rd 1865

My Dear Wash

Our little town is almost entirely deserted today, and every thing seems
so still and quiet, that I can almost imagine myself in the country. The
pic-nic, of which I spoke in one of my former letters, takes place today, in
a woods about a mile from town, and nearly every one in the surrounding neighborhood has gone to it. As for myself I prefered rational enjoyment at home, to being mixed up in such a crowd. Of course they are
to dance, as that seems to be the order of the day at present. I think it
very wrong for members of the church to go to such public places and
dance, although last Winter I was guilty of the sin myself, but I suffered
enough for it. I have never been able to forgive myself for it. Although I
trust I have obtained forgiveness from a Higher power. I am so fond of
the amusement that I find it very hard to resist the temptation. Fannie
does not think it wrong, consequently she attends the pic-nic's &c. Last
Wednesday Harriot, Fannie, another young lady and myself with Maj.
Beall as our driver started for cousin Hugh Pendleton's on a cherrying[24]
expedition, and on our way had such a serious adventure, that we were
detained all night. You ought to have been along, and you would have
had an opportunity of displaying a good deal of heroism. H. gave cousin
Richard a full account of the transaction in her last letter, so it is not
worthwhile to enter into details, suffice it to say that but for the determined courage of our gallant little driver, we might all have found a
watery grave.

I have received three letters from you this week, two yesterday. Heretofore you had better direct your letters simply to Smithfield, Jefferson Co
via Kearneysville,[25] B & O R. R.[26] Va. I am glad you are so hopeful about
your release, and sincerely hope you may not be disappointed.

You have a cheerful disposition, or surely you could not stand your imprisonment so well. I was ever hopeful and confident of the future, but
my faith has been very much shaken by the late occurrences.

---

24. That is, picking cherries.

25. Located in West Virginia, fewer than ten miles from Sharpsburg, Md.

26. The Baltimore & Ohio Railroad linked Washington, D.C., and the Midwest and was,
therefore, a crucial supply line for the Union. James McPherson, *Battle Cry of Freedom: The
Civil War Era* (Oxford, England: Oxford University Press, 1988), 299.

I rarely ever indulge in that propensity to which I used to be so prone in my *youthful days* viz. "building castles in the air,"[27] for they have all been so completely demolished, that now, I never look beyond today. Encourage your cheerful spirit. You will be much happier for it. We have an opportunity to [visit] Charlottesville next week, and Aunt Fannie has written to your Ma, hoping the letter may reach her in safety. I suppose communication is open by this time. Mrs. Massie is indeed a kind friend. Such are worth possessing. I wish she was powerful enough to get you out of prison. From the description I have had of Fort Delaware it must be very unpleasant there this warm weather. Sitting here in the parlor I feel scarcely equal to the exertion of writing a letter probably however my dull feelings are owing to fatigue.

Our cook has left us, and Harriot and myself have to be the house-cleaners, which is a very tiresome occupation in the Summer time. It is very provoking that all my letters come to me open. I always feel as if they have been read, which deprives me of much pleasure that I would otherwise experience in reading them myself. However as I cannot remedy the matter, it is useless to complain.

I am glad you have heard from home. Do give much love to them *all* from us, when you write, Tell cousin Richard we are glad to hear that he can be persuaded to do right. We shall certainly expect him with you. All send love to you and himself. May Heavens richest blessings descend upon you. Good bye.

Mollie

Wash was released from prison in June 1865 and, according to the next letter, had visited Mollie in late June or early July. The following letter, addressed to Beaver Dam Depot in Hanover County, Virginia, suggests that some letters between the two were lost or intentionally destroyed.

Middleburg July 12th, 1865

My Dear Wash,

I was sitting at Aunt Betsy's yesterday morning, and had just remarked to Fan that I felt as though I would get a letter, when Harriot came in, and handed me yours. Having read and replaced it in the envelope, the company inquired the Hanover news, where upon I replied that there

---

27. A popular attitude in the antebellum era about the trouble-free period of youth.

was none, at which they seemed much chagrined and thought it very
selfish in you to write such a long letter, and not give any news. After
a time however, I managed to appease their wrath by reading to them
the *readable* parts. I am indeed sorry to have been the cause of so much
disappointment of the good people of Hanover, and also that Aunt Jane
should have taken on so much useless trouble. You must tell her how
highly I appreciate her kind intentions. Perhaps some day we may take
advantage of their hospitality.

And you got that letter did you? I was in hopes by some accident or
other it might have been destroyed, for I remember how *foolishly* I had
expressed myself, and no sooner had it reached the office than I re-
gretted having written it, however "what's done can't be undone," so I
suppose I must abide the consequences, and trust to your kind heart for
forgiveness. It was written during the War, and then you know all ladies
were more or less demoralized. I know exactly what you will say when
you read this, so you need not in your next letter attempt to convince me
that I am wrong. Really Wash you are becoming so reckless of your life
that I shall be afraid for you to travel alone, however after having passed
unscathed through Yankee hands, I think you must be destined to die a
natural death. And now I expect you would like to know what I have been
doing with myself since your departure. The evening of the day you left
we were invited to spend at Mr Myers'. I went, and of course had a very
dull time. The following Friday we accepted our invitation to Mr Camp-
bell's, and enjoyed the visit very much. In the evening a storm coming
up compelled us to stay all night, which circumstances we did not regret.
When we returned next day, we found Robert Pendleton here. His plan
about the school has fallen through. We are disappointed as well as himself. In the evening of the same day I received your letter from Balt. I
read it in the parlor, and actually it was so demonstrative that it made me
blush. However *of course I* could make all due allowances. What does Aunt
Jane think of our plans for the future or have you told her of them? How
will she like the idea of your coming up here to live? I hope you may not
be gifted with the power to "put time on telegraph wires between this and
the middle of Oct." for there is so much to do and think about in these
three months, that I hardly think I have given myself time enough.

Well! I have written so far, and have not even mentioned how terribly
I missed you after you left, however as a matter of course I suppose you
took it for granted you would be missed in a slight degree.

I was sorry you forgot your overcoat, hope you did not need it on
the way.

I have taken the buttons and trimming off your uniform coat to have it washed, then I shall put it away, and after the middle of Oct, if you say so, I intend to turn it, and make a new coat of it.

Does Berkeley intend accepting Aunt Adelaide's[28] offer. Aunt Betsey wishes he would that they might send Tom Mann to him. Perhaps we might get occasional sight of him, though Long Branch seems almost out of the world to us, and I believe they think the same of Smithfield. The day after you left, I received a note from Sister Annie, containing a cravat for "dear Wash." She doesn't think it very suitable, as the color is green, but nevertheless it is very pretty. I shall keep it until you come, fearing to risk it in a letter. She was disappointed at not seeing you but was prevented from coming up by the illness of her little girl. H. and I walked down last week and staid a night, and the next day went to pay a visit to Mrs Callaway. I am so glad you met with our dear old pastor. We are expecting them up the last of the month to spend some time with us, when I expect to enjoy the services. It has been so long since I had the privilege of attending my own church. The misses Francis arrived yesterday evening. I have not seen them yet, but shall call on them as soon as possible. It has been raining incessantly all day. Can you hear nothing from Uncle Francis family? We are so anxious about Sister Lizzie. You need not be afraid of trying my eyes with crossed letters.[29] I do not object to them, and you cannot make your letters too long for me. You know we cannot hear very often from each other, so you must make up in length for the deficiency in numbers. Do give my best love to dear Aunt Judy. How I envy you that morning at Oakland. My love to Aunt Jane and cousin Jennie, and all my other relations. You may take a *little bit* for yourself. You ask me to say that I love you, and then again you are convinced, that I do. Well, if you are convinced, let the matter rest. There is no need for me to strengthen the conviction. All join me in great deal of love to each member of your household. Has Frank returned from college.[30] Good bye. Write again soon to your devoted

   Mollie

The letter from Richmond I did not receive

Patsey asked me to inquire if her father is still living.

---

28. Adelaide Holker Nelson was Mollie's aunt; she lived at Long Branch Plantation. Her husband, Hugh Mortimer Nelson (Sr.), was killed at Gaines Mill in 1862.

29. "Crossed letters," or cross-hatched writing, refers to reorienting the page after it has been written on and continuing to write on the same page in a perpendicular direction.

30. In the Civil War era, it was not uncommon for a fourteen- or fifteen-year-old male youth such as Frank to attend college, so long as he passed entrance examinations.

Mount Air[31] Sept 4th 65

Like you, my darling Mollie, I have been interrupted in writing by company, so much so that in two weeks I have written you only two letters. I made a desperate effort last Friday after a ride, *muleback*, of thirty miles that day and fifty the day before to get a letter ready to send off Saturday; I had just told you of my broken down condition, and assured you that if I went writing to any one else I was sure I would go to sleep over my paper. And I was intensely disgusted on waking about two hours afterwards to find I had already been to sleep over a letter to you. I had thought it impossible for the flesh to triumph over the spirit in such a case, but "tired nature's sweet restorer"[32] would have its way—it enticed me with sweet dreams and ones with you believing I saw you and heard you speak, how could I wake?

I am much comforted by your permission to write "anything and everything" I please, I don't expect to use it fully, but it is a great satisfaction to know I will be safe in whatever I *may* say. I spend a portion of every day mentally ransacking a confectionary shop for names sweet enough to embody my idea. I have not succeeded in half satisfying myself, but expect I would "overwhelm["][33] you in spite of yourself were I to give you the benefit of my efforts. Any way I am afraid to try it. You tell me you intend to be as "willful as possible" for the next month & a half, so I dare not venture much. I will wait until we are safely married, and then when I want to get you to listen to what I have to say or to tell me something I want to know, I will get the Bible and read you where it says, wife obey your husband. I am glad you count upon "walking straight" next winter, as I expect you will keep me pretty straight, and I rather be taught by example than precept. Why, my love, do you determine to talk no more about so interesting a subject as our marriage until October? Is it that you

31. A plantation in northern Virginia (now an historic site in Fairfax County), established by the McCarty family in the early eighteenth century. Because it was located along the Confederate and Union border, the armies of both governments used it to obtain supplies. Ultimately, the Union army occupied the estate. See Christopher Daniel, "Mount Air: Former Homestead Tied to Fort Belvoir History," *U.S. Army*, Feb. 1, 2010, http://www.army .mil/article/33827/mount-air-former-homestead-tied-to-fort-belvoir-history.

32. From Edward Young's immensely popular poem "Night Thoughts" (1742–45). See Edward Young, *Night Thoughts on Life, Death, and Mortality* (Philadelphia: Published by John Stevenson, Anderson & Mechan, printers, 1820). The whole line reads "Tired nature's sweet restorer, balmy sleep!"

33. It is unclear in the original manuscript where this quotation ended because Wash did not include a final quotation mark. Regardless, Wash seems to be quoting parts of previous letters of which there are no extant copies.

think it too delightful to be talked about? You seem to give me credit for no curiosity at all or maybe you think not to satisfy it is good discipline for me. Well, I must submit to your judgment. Only let me love you, and love me a little in return, and I will be as pliant as clay. I understand my orders are not to come up until the Saturday before the 17th. I suppose you mean to exclude me only for Smithfield up to that time—Jennie wants to pay a visit at Longbranch on our way up. So I expect to be in the Valley about the last of the 1st week in October. You can endure me twenty miles off can't you? The temptation to take a pass at you before Saturday will be tremendous. May I go to church with you the next day? And won't you give me a heap of extra kisses to pay me for having stayed away so long?

Is Mr. Gibson, of whom you spoke, an Episcopal minister? You speak of him as "our new minister." If so, how will we do about asking Mr. Calloway to marry us? One minister generally does not like another to marry a couple in his parish. I have always heard they are very sensitive on such points. I would like to know the form of the *story* you told Miss Sallie Dandridge[.] Somebody is constantly asking me such questions, and I am often "posed" for an answer. I remember I used to admire the face with which my friend Rhodes Massie derived such things. He would look you in the face, and tell you in the most earnest manner, that there was not a bit of truth in anything you had heard. Berkely staid with me last night. I delivered your message about Miss Mamie Bates, but it did not seem to affect him very much. I can't tell you that something else about him now, but I assure you it is not because I wish to follow your example, for it would never do for both of us to be "obstinate" at the same time. I would willingly gratify your curiosity if it weren't for a promise I am under to Berkely. I will tell you after we are married. You will I reckon enjoy it, just as much, and I won't run any risk then. I told you sometime since I would never mention Willie Rounquist[34] unless at your request, but I have a bit of news about him which I think ought not to be kept from you. He proposes taking unto himself a wife; his sister told Jennie [that] William was fully determined to have a wife, though he had not made up his mind whom he would however, but anyhow he intended to "get a gal that had a home" and hearing that Miss Jones, on whom he waited at church, had said he was the prettiest young man she ever did see, and she being a "gal that had a home" he led a strong notion to "set his snares" in her direction. I might go on and speak of this victim to your charms at length

---

34. William P. Rounquist of Hanover County, Va., who served in the Virginia Light Artillery during the Civil War.

finding consolation, or I might describe him in despair at the approach
of your marriage, throwing himself away upon the first woman who could
give him a home, but I forbear. I remember my promise, and will make
no comments. I must touch upon another forbidden subject, "Fruit," just
to call your attention to the fact that you missed all this, by not coming
down with me in July, just think of the fruit the "soldier" would have gotten for his darling wife. I have been offered a "cart load" of water melons
any time I may go for them and you ought to be here for me to supply
them at your feet. How I would enjoy eating one with you! I imagine myself cutting a great big slice for my wife, bless her heart she might have
the whole melon. Never mind. I will have a chance to cut water melons
and pull peaches for you yet. I am mightily sorry to hear that Butler has
inflammatory Rheumatism, I know what agony it is, and can feel for any
one who has it. Ma is really sick. She has not been out of her bed for six
days. She took violent cold in some way I am really uneasy about her. We
have a case of Diphtheria too—Mammy has been very sick with it, but is
better now. Jennie has her hands full with Ma & Mammy both sick. The
boys are well again, and are now going to school to Charley Minor. Mrs
Massie is expected at Edgewood about the middle of this month, I look
forward to meeting her with much pleasure. I stopped writing a while ago
to speak to a negro boy, speaking to him only produced impertinence, so
I had to resort to stronger measures. He resisted with all his might, and
being a big strong boy, I had a good deal of trouble. It was the worse for
him though, as I had to knock him down, and I hit a pretty hard lick. His
Daddy & Mammy were both by, and seemed inclined at first to take up
the quarrel, but I advised them not, as I should certainly kill them if they
did, and they took my advice. I have no time to write so long a letter as I
would wish now, love, but I will write again soon. Jennie sends her "very
best" love, says she looks for a letter from you. Good bye, dearest Mollie,
a hundred kisses to you. Your own
    Wash

September 25th 1865—At Home[35]

My dear Wash
    I expect by this time you are beginning to wonder what in the world
has become of me, and to accuse me of obstinacy, willfulness and all such

---

35. Letter is directed to Wash in the care of General Pendleton, Gettysburg, Pa.

horrible traits, but I assure it was not my intention to impress you with any such opinion of me, for my seeming neglect has been unavoidable. Week before the last I sent you the regular missive, but last week I was so much engaged with company and other duties that I had no opportunity of writing. Some days [I] was compelled even to neglect reading my Bible. I am glad for one reason that the 17th of Oct. is so near at hand, and it is, that this abominable practice of writing letters will then be stopped. Sometimes, when I am in the humor for it, and have nothing else to do, it gives me pleasure to communicate my thoughts to another, but to be compelled to write a letter at a certain time, even though it be to *you*, whether I feel like it or not, often proves a task rather than a pleasure. Had I the pen of a ready writer, of course I should have no antipathy to the custom, but after reading your letters, and noticing the fluency and ease with which you exercise your feelings and ideas, I often feel reproached for sending you such indifferent productions as mine always are, but I know you do not "view them with the critic's eye," which is a great consolation. I have always heard that "love is blind," and I think it must be so in this instance, for I can't see what there is in me to call forth such love and admiration from any one. Every day I feel my imperfections more and more and more, and your superiority in every respect, but I do not wish to feel otherwise, for I would not marry a man unless he were my superior. I should not respect him and how could I love one whom I did not respect. I often wonder how any woman of intelligence can marry a man deficient in that respect, and one instance is constantly before me, at which I shall never cease to wonder, if it ever takes place, and I think it will, but "de gustibus non disputandum est."[36] This day three weeks you will all be here, Providence permitting, and every thing I suppose will be arranged for the following day.

I think we can make the arrangement to have Tom Mann as one of the actors, so I shall let him know of your intention. You and your groomsmen are to stay at Aunt Betsey's, as we will have a house full of company. Aunt Fannie paid last week the long talked of visit to "Long Branch." They spoke often of you all, and seem delighted at the prospect of seeing you there so soon. Cousin Nannie has made all arrangements to bring you down. She sent me a nice present, one that I little expected from her, but I suppose it was for your sake, and not mine. Aunt Fannie saw Henry, who told her that he had been sent there to wait until your arrival.

---

36. The Latin translates into English as "there is nothing to dispute concerning literary taste."

You must write and tell me what day you intend starting [to travel], so that I may know whether to write again. If you leave the first of Oct a letter would not have time to reach you, so perhaps this may be the last that I shall write. I have not written to Mr Callaway yet, but shall do so soon. Fannie seems to think that he expects me to call upon him to perform the ceremony.

Our minister, Mr Gibson was formerly a Methodist minister, and has lately applied for orders in our church, but as he has never been ordained, of course he would not be privileged to tie the knot for us. Cousin Lizzie Pendleton and Robert spent a day and night with us last week. The latter leaves for Washington College[37] on the coming Wednesday. He is in high spirits and thinks his prospects for the future bright, he had a few days before placed the engagement ring upon the finger of his lady-love miss Jane Blackburn, and thinks himself very safe now. Dudley is as gay as a lark, doesn't seem to mind his repulse at all. Give my love to Berkeley, and tell him I wish him better success with the young lady than others have had.

We are expecting Lella Pendleton the latter part of this week, to pay me a visit. It will be rather inconvenient to have her just at this time, but of course we shall do all in our power to make her enjoy herself as much as possible. Fan returned from Balt. on Thursday. She goes tomorrow to act as bridesmaid for Fannie Griggs who is to be married tomorrow night. Lizzie will not be at home before the first of next month. She has paid a long visit. I am sorry to hear of Sanny Minors ill health. Give her my love also to the rest of the family. I hope cousin Jennie's flesh and appetite will return when she comes to the valley. Love from all to your house hold. Hoping to see you soon. I am as ever yours and yours only

    Mollie. N. Scollay

I have written to cousin Nannie to be one of my brides maids.

    I send some stamps.

---

37. Now Washington and Lee University, located in Lexington, Va.

CHAPTER 6

"A Dark Record of Suffering and Oppression"

Wash Nelson's Memoir

After the war, Confederate veterans and their sympathizers struggled to understand defeat. In particular, they wondered how God would allow "the Yankees"—whom they perceived as a morally inferior people—to achieve victory over the morally superior South. After men returned from army and prison life, their experiences haunted them, and we see the specter of war vividly in the following story Wash wrote in 1866 about his captivity. Juxtaposed with his letters, the memoir is a portal into the uneven transition from experience to memory, war to peace, and from anecdotal epistle to narrative. In this chapter, both what Wash mentions and omits are important.

Prison life

I was captured on the 26th October 1863 under the following circumstances. I had just returned from within the enemy's lines to my companion's home on the border.[1]

We were eating dinner and thought ourselves perfectly secure. The sight of a blue coat at the window was our first intimation of the presence of the Yankees. We immediately jumped up and ran into another room, expecting to escape through a back window, but to our dismay found this outlet guarded also.

We next made tremendous exertions to get up into the garret of the house, but the trap door was so weighted down as to resist our utmost

---

1. According to his military service records, Nelson was captured on October 26, 1863, and "arrested" the following day in New Market, Va.

strength. The effort to double up our long legs in a wardrobe was equally unsuccessful, at last we threw ourselves under a bed and awaited our fate.

A few minutes—and in they came—swords clattering—pistols cocked and levelled. They soon spied our legs under the bed—"Come out of that" was yelled out, then pistols were put in our faces and I heard several voices call out "Surrender"! which we did, with as good a grace as we could. There was no other course left. It would have been madness to resist so large a force, and every chance for "a run" was cut off.

It was mortifying in the extreme to surrender without one blow for liberty, but recognizing the necessity, we yielded. The ladies of the house were much distressed and alarmed, particularly when the Yankees came up to us with their pistols levelled. They implored—"Don't shoot them, don't shoot them" The Yankees answered—"O We ain't a going to hurt them[.]"

A few minutes were given us to say goodbye. Then we were put upon our horses, (which they had found) placed in the column with a trooper on each side, and one in front of us leading our horses, thus precluding all chance of escape.

We had gone about a mile, when an Orderly came up to us with an order from the Colonel to bring the ranking prisoner to the head of the column. Accordingly I was led forward. The Colonel saluted me, and introducing a Captain Bailey who was riding with him, said we should be treated with all possible courtesy while in his charge. I will do him the justice to say—he kept this word.

He then proceeded to question me about our army. There were very few questions of this kind which I would have answered, but it happened that the Colonel and myself were both quite deaf,[2] which gave rise to a ludicrous mistake and resulted in putting a stop to the catechism.

Question—"Does Jeff Davis visit the army often?" Answer "O, yes, while we were camped about Orange Courthouse, the array of beauty was great, and the smiles of the fair ones fully compensated for the hardships of the Pennsylvania Campaign."

I thought he asked me whether the ladies visited the army.

He asked me what I said. I repeated. I then noticed he had a puzzled look, and that Captain Bailey could hardly restrain his laughter. So I told him I was deaf and had probably misunderstood his question. He an-

---

2. There is no evidence to suggest that Wash was deaf, or even hard of hearing.

A group of Union soldiers interrogate a Confederate prisoner
early in the conflict. Alfred A. Waud, *Provost Marshal—and police of
Alexandria searching and examining a prisoner of war, 1861*, Library
of Congress, https://www.loc.gov/item/2004660107/.

swered that he was deaf too. I came to the conclusion he thought I was
quizzing, as he asked no more questions.

It is my intention to give full credit for every kindness, for stretched
to the utmost, they are but two or three bright spots in a dark record
of suffering and oppression. One of these occurred the evening of our
capture. I had no gloves and the night was very cold. Captain Bail[e]y
seeing this, gave me one of his and the next day brought me a pair he
had gotten for me.

We halted the first night at a place called Ninneveh.[3] We were put
for safe keeping in a small outhouse, where we made our bed upon
"squashes" and broken pieces of an old stove, this did not trouble us
however as we intended to watch all night for a chance to escape. But a
numerous and vigilant guard disappointed us.

---

3. A misspelling of the town Nineveh, Va., which is located approximately forty-six miles
northeast of New Market, Va.

We reached Strasburg[4] the next evening where our captors gave us a
dinner. We then went on to Winchester where we spent the night. The
Yankee Officers gave us a firstrate [*sic*] supper. We reached Charlestown
next day where dinner was again given us, a very good one too. The Yankee Officers took us to their mess and treated us very courteously. That
evening, the Colonel commanding, took us to Harper's Ferry.[5] As we
were starting, Captain Bailey very kindly gave us some tobacco, remark-
ing "You will find some difficulty in getting such things on the way.["]

The Colonel left us at the Ferry, and we found ourselves in the hands
of a very different set of men. We were put in the "John Brown Engine
House"[6] where were already some twenty five or thirty prisoners. There
were no beds, no seats, and the walls and floor were alive with lice. Before
being sent to this hole we were stripped and searched. We staid here
about thirty six hours, were then sent on to Wheeling[7] where our lodg-
ing was neither so small nor so lousy as the one we had left, but the
company was even less to our taste than lice, viz Yankee convicts. We
remained here two or three days and were then taken to Camp Chase.[8]
We got there in the night, were cold and wet. After undergoing a considerable amount of cursing and abuse, we were turned into Prison No.
1 to shift for ourselves as best we could. At Camp Chase, I made my first
attempt at washing clothes. Having no change, I had to be minus shirt,
drawers, and socks during the operation. I worked so hard as to rub
all the skin off my knuckles, and yet not enough to get the dirt out of
my garments. We stayed at this place about twenty days. We were then
started off for Johnson's Island[.] My friend had ten dollars, good money,
when we reached Camp Chase, which was taken from him and Sutler's
checks given instead. When we were to leave for Johnson's Island, where
of course, Camp Chase checks would be useless, the Sutler made it convenient not to be on hand to redeem his paper, so my Friend lost all the
little money he had.

---

4. Wash's memory of geography is off here. Nineveh is farther north than Strasburg,
which is right off present day I-81. A slight drop down to Strasburg, however, is not exceed-
ingly far out of the way Wash describes, so it is not an unbelievable route.

5. Harpers Ferry was the site of the abolitionist John Brown's famous raid on the federal
armory in 1859, which greatly exacerbated sectional tensions between the North and the
South.

6. Also called John Brown's fort, where John Brown took fellow raiders when he realized
capture was imminent. When Brown refused to surrender, the fort was stormed by U.S.
marines, and he and his men were captured and imprisoned.

7. Wheeling, W.Va.

8. Union prison established west of Columbus, Ohio, in May 1861.

We were marched from Camp Chase to Columbus,[9] where we took the cars. This march was brutally conducted. Several of our number were sick and yet the whole party was made to double quick nearly the entire distance of five miles. We traveled all day, reached Johnson's Island in the night, worn out and hungry. I was at Johnson's Island from about Nov. 20th to April 26th[.] During this time, I suffered a great deal, in common with many others. Prisoners who were supplied by friends in the North, got along very well, but those altogether dependent upon the tender mercies of the government, were poorly off indeed. I was in this latter class for some time, not being able to communicate with my friends, until the beginning of the New Year. The building in which I lived on Johnson's Island, was a simple, weather-boarded house, through which the bleak wind blew, and the snow beat at will. It is true that many of the buildings were quite comfortable, but I speak of my own experience.

The 1st of January 1864 was said by all to be the coldest weather ever known at that point. It was so cold that the Sentinels were taken off—for fear of their freezing. Whenever the air struck the face, the sensation was that of ice pressed hard against it. Yet cold as it was, we were without fire in my room from three o clock P.M. to nine next morning. I went to my bed which consisted of two blankets, one to lie upon—and one to cover with, but sleep was out of the question, in such circumstances. So I got up, got together several fellow prisoners, and kept up—the circulation of blood and their spirits, until daylight, by dancing. My chum, unfortunately, staid in our bunk—and in consequence, he was so badly frost bitten that he could not get on his boots.

During my sojourn in this prison, there was at times, a scarcity of water, sufficient to cause not merely inconvenience, but often actual suffering among us.

The wells from which we got our supply, were shallow and we generally exhausted them early in the afternoon. A lake of water surrounded us, whence we might have been allowed a plentiful supply, but the fear of our escaping was so great, that we were never allowed to go to the lake, except through a long line of guards. This opportunity was given once a day, unless the wells were frozen, so that no water could be had from them at all, then we had access to the lake twice a day.

In this prison, in common with all others, in which it was my misfortune to be confined, we were liable to be shot at, at any time, for every

---

9. Columbus, Ohio.

thing and for nothing. I remember three different times my room was fired into, at night because the Sentinel said we had lights burning, when to my certain knowledge, there was no light in the room. The authorities had rules struck up, the observance of which would ensure safety, they said. It is true their nonoberservance could almost certainly, entail death or a wound, but the converse was by no means true. Sentinels interpreted rules as they pleased—and fired upon us at the dictates of their own cowardly hearts. In no instance have I ever heard of their being punished for it, though it was clearly proven that the sufferer had violated no rule. This prison afforded opportunity for the exhibition of a spirit characteristic of our people, and which now that they are overpowered and under the heel of oppression—is still manifest. It is a spirit at once self reliant and submissive to the will of Providence, which added to conscious nobility of purpose, in what would else be ignominy, gives brave men dignity, and bids them make the best of their surroundings. This spirit showed itself at Johnson's Island in the efforts made to pass the time. School-clubs, and games of all kinds were established. There were shops of every description. The blacksmith, shoemaker, tailor, jeweler, &c. each carried on his respective trade. The impression is on my mind of many disagreeable, unkind and oppressive measures taken by the authorities, with regard to our pursuits, but the very severe treatment to which I was afterwards subjected so far threw them into the shade, that the particulars escape my recollection.

I must not omit a statement about food. At Camp Chase, my rations were of good quality and enough. At Johnson's Island—they were not so good nor near so plentiful, though sufficient to keep a man in health. I made two efforts to escape from Johnson's Island. My first attempt was in the month of December. I begun a tunnel from under one of the buildings with the intention of coming to the surface, outside the pen surrounding the prison. My intention then was to swim to the nearest point of mainland, about a quarter of a mile distant and then make across the country for the South. I had with infinite labour during three of four nights made a considerable hole, and was in spirits at the prospect, when one night there came a tremendous rain, which caved in my tunnel and blasted my hopes for that time. Six of us were engaged in this effort.

My next attempt was on the 2nd of June 1864,[10] during the intensely cold weather I succeeded in getting to the fence where the sentinel was

---

10. Wash was at Point Lookout, not Johnson's Island, on June 2, 1864. Given the comment about the cold weather, he may have meant January 2.

posted, but the guard was so vigilant, it was impossible to get over. I lay by the fence until I was almost frozen, then the moon shone out brightly, and I had to run for my life.

Early in the Spring of '64, the two governments agreed upon an exchange of sick and disabled prisoners. I had been sick for some three months, accordingly I went before the board of Physicians which decided that I was a fit subject for exchange.

On the 26th of April, in company with 140 sick, I left Johnson's Island, fully believing that in a few days—I should be once more in dear old Dixie. We traveled by rail to Baltimore, and thence by Steamer to Pt. Lookout. Here I drank to the dregs the cup of "Hope deferred which maketh the heart sick."[11] Every few days, we were told, we would certainly leave for the South by the next boat. Once we were all actually called up to sign the parole, "not to take up arms &c, until regularly exchanged" but the order was countermanded before one third of us had signed the roll. I have never, before or since, felt so sick at heart as then. My disappointments of the same character have been many—but this overtopped them all. All faith in the truthfulness of any Government official was then forever shattered. Hereafter Hope as is her wont, would spring eternal in the human breast, but never felt herself securely perched. A fall was always expected. The greater part of my time at Point Lookout was passed in the Hospital, where I was very well treated. The sick were not closely guarded and had the privilege of the whole point. It was no small consolation to sit for hours on the beach, the fresh breeze blowing in your face, and the free water rolling before you—moodful as nature's own child, sparking with infinite lustre, in the sunshine of a calm day— kissing the breeze with soft murmurs of welcome, or struggling with an angry war in the embrace of the tempest. Eight miles distant was the Virginia shore, and I have often thought I might claim a kindred feeling with the prophet, viewing from Horeb the land he might not enter.[12] About the middle of May—the Hospital was crowded with wounded Yankees sent from Butler's lines.[13] This necessitated our removal, accordingly

---

11. Proverbs 13:12: "Hope deferred maketh the heart sick: but *when* the desire cometh, *it is* a tree of life."

12. Allusion to the Hebrew prophet Elijah, who fled into the wilderness to Mount Horeb, where God appeared to him. 1 Kings 19.

13. Possibly a reference to the Bermuda Hundred Campaign (May 12–16, 1864), near Richmond, Va., wherein U.S. major general Benjamin Butler led the Army of the James closer toward Richmond before Confederate general P. G. T. Beauregard stopped the Union advance.

we were sent out to the regular prison. There we lived in tents. We still had one luxury—sea bathing. The drinking water here was very injurious, causing diarrhea. About this time rations were reduced. We were cut down to two meals a day—Coffee and Sugar were stopped. The ration was a *small* loaf of bread per day, a small piece of meat for breakfast, meat and soup—so called—for dinner. About the 20th of June I was removed to Fort Delaware.[14] We were crowded in the hold and between decks of a steamer for three days, the time occupied in the trip. I thought it was terrible at the time but subsequent experience taught me that it was a small matter. On reaching Fort Delaware, we underwent the "search" usual at most prisons—what money I had, I wrapped in brown paper—which I enclosed in a chew of tobacco and put in my mouth. I thus managed to secure it. An insufficiency of food was the chief complaint at Fort Delaware. I did not suffer. My friends supplied me with money, and I purchased from a Sutler what I needed. While at Fort Delaware, one of our number, Col. James of Va, was murdered by the guard. Col. James had been sick for some time, one foot was so swollen he could not bear a shoe upon it, and it was with difficulty he walked at all; One evening he hobbled to "the Sinks." As he was about to return, a considerable crowd of prisoners collected there. The Sentinel ordered them to move off— which they did. Col James could not move fast. The Sentinel ordered him to move faster. He replied that he was doing the best he could, he could not walk any faster. Whereupon the Sentinel shot him, the ball passing through the arm and lungs. He lived about 24 hours. He remarked to the Commandant of the Post, "Sir, I am a murdered man, murdered for nothing. I was breaking no rule." The prisoners at Fort Delaware were great beer drinkers. Their beer was made of molasses and water and sold by prisoners to each other at 5 cents a glass.

Beer was drunk instead of water, the latter article being very warm, and at times very brackish. At Fort Delaware, we were kept on the rack by alternative hope and disappointment. Rumors that never came to anything—of an immediate general exchange, were everyday occurrences.

On the 20th of August 1864 six hundred of us were selected and sent to Morris Island in Charleston Harbor to be placed under the fire of our own batteries.

We started in high spirits, for we firmly believed, we were soon to be exchanged for a like number of the enemy in Charleston. In some in-

---

14. Service records document Wash's transfer to Fort Delaware as occurring on June 23, 1864.

stances men gave their gold watches to some of the "lucky ones" as we were termed, to be allowed to go in their places.

On the evening of the 20th we were all six hundred stowed away between the decks of the Steamer "Crescent." Bunks had been prepared for us. These were arranged in three tiers along the whole length of the ship. Two rows of three tiers on each side of the ship, leaving a very narrow passage way—So narrow that two men could with difficulty squeeze by each other. In the centre of the rows, the lower and centre tiers of bunks were shrouded in continual night. The little light the port holes being shut out by the upper tiers of bunks.

My bunk which was about five feet, ten inches square, and occupied by four persons, was right against the boiler, occasioning an additional amount of heat, which made the sensation of suffocation almost unbearable. Here we lay in these bunks, packed away like sardines in all 15 days in the hottest part of summer. In two instances, the guard placed in with us fainted. I heard one of them remark, "A dog couldnt stand this."

Perspiration rolled from us in streams all the time, clothes and blankets were saturated with it and it dripped constantly from the upper to the lower bunks. Our sufferings were aggravated by a scarcity of water. The water furnished us was condensed, and the thirst for it was so intense, that it was taken from the condenser almost boiling hot, and drunk in that state. One evening during a rain we were allowed on deck, several of us carried up an old dirty oil cloth which we held by the four corners until nearly full of rain water. We then plunged our heads in, and drank to our fill. I remember well the sensation of delight—the wild joy with which I felt the cool water about my face and going down my throat.

On one occasion, hearing that the surgeon gave his medicines in ice water, I went to him and asked for a dose of "Salts" which he gave me— and after it a glass of ice water. He remarked upon the indifference with which I swallowed the physic. I told him I would take another dose for another glass of ice water, which he was kind enough to give me minus the salts. It is strange that none of us died during the trip, I can account for it only by the fact that we were all sustained by the strong hope of a speedy exchange and home. Our skins were much tanned, when we started, bleached as white as possible during this trip. We lay for some days off Port Royal,[15] while a pen was being made for us on Morris Island, in which to confine us. While at Anchor three of our number attempted

---

15. Located in the South Carolina low country.

to escape. They found some life preservers, somewhere in the ship. With these they got overboard in the night, swam some eight or ten miles, where two of them landed. The third man kept on swimming and I never heard of him afterwards. The other two got lost among the islands and arms of the sea, and after scuffling and suffering for three days, were recaptured and brought back to their old quarters. On the 7th September, 1864 we landed on Morris Island. We disembarked during the middle of the day, under a scorching sun, but even this change from the close, and by this time filthy hold of the ship was delightful. During the voyage we were guarded by white soldiers. These were now exchanged for blacks— and they were certainly the blackest I ever saw. But black, uncouth and barbarous as they were, we soon found that they were far preferable to the white officers who commanded them. If physiognomy be any index of character, then certainly those officers were villainous. But not one of them in looks for deeds could compare with their Colonel. Sure am I that if Satan has upon earth choice ministers of his diabolical will, that man was one of them. I always felt in his presence as if I had suddenly come upon a snake. He used frequently to come into the pen and talk with some of the prisoners, he seemed to take a fiendish pleasure in our sufferings. A prisoner said to him, on one occasion, "Colonel, unless you give us more to eat we will starve." His reply was "If I had my way, I would feed you upon an oiled rag." Once he told us, we must bury the refuse bones &c in the sand, to prevent any bad smell from them. One of the prisoners answered, "If you don't give us something more to eat, there will be nothing to bury, and none of us left to bury it."

"Ah well"! he replied, "when you commence to *stink*, I'll put you in the ground too." The bread issued us was spoiled, and filled with worms. Some one remonstrated with him about giving men such stuff to eat. His answer was, "You were complaining about not having any fresh meat, so I thought I would supply you."

The pen in which we were confined, had an area of about one square acre. It was nearly mid way between Batteries Gregg & Wagner,[16] perfectly exposed to the shot and shell fired at the two Batteries. The principal firing was from mortars and was done mostly at night. We lived in tents and had not the least protection from the fire. This however, troubled us little. Our great concern was at the small amount and desperate quality of the food issued.

---

16. Two Confederate batteries on Morris Island, S.C.

One of our greatest pleasures was to watch the shells at night, darting through the air like shooting stars, and in predicting how near to us they would explode. Sometimes they exploded just overhead and the fragments went whizzing all about us. But strange to say, during our stay there, from Sept 7th to Octo 19th not one of our number was struck, though there was firing every day and night and some times it was very brisk. The negro guard was as much exposed as ourselves. One of them had his leg knocked off by a shell, the only person struck, that I know of. In this place we lived in a small A tents[17] four men to a tent. The heat was intense during the day, but the nights were cool and pleasant.

The only drawback to sleep being the constant noise of exploding shell, and the firing of the Forts by us. Our camp was laid off in streets, two rows of tents facing each other making a street. These rows were called A, B, C, D, E, F, G, & H. A negro Sergeant had charge of each row calling it "his company[.]" His duties were to call the roll three times a day, issue rations, and exercise a general superintendence. These Sergeants were generally kind to us—Expressed their sorrow that we had so little to eat. We had a point in common with them, viz[.] intense hatred of their Colonel. His treatment of them, for the least violation of orders, or infraction of discipline was barbarous.

He would ride at them, knock and beat them over the head with his sabre, or draw his pistol and shoot at them.

Our rations were issued in manner and quantity as follows—The Sergeant came around to each tent with a box of hard biscuit and issued to each prisoner, three biscuit generally, sometimes two, sometimes one and a half, towards the last of our stay, five were issued—which number was what the authorities allowed us. The Sergeant next came round with a box of small slices of meat about the length and width of two fingers, one of these was given to each man. This was breakfast. At dinner time, the Sergeant went round with a barrel of "pea soup" and gave each man from a third to half a pint. Supper time was marked by the issue of a little mush or rice, this too was brought around in a barrel. I have mentioned the *lively* nature of the bread, any one who had not seen it, would hardly credit the amount of dead animal matter, in the shape of white worms, which was in the mush given us.

For my own part, I was always too hungry to be dainty, worms, mush and all went to relieve the cravings of nature. But I knew several fastidi-

---

17. The "A," or "wedge," tent, unlike tents soldiers carried on campaign, was large enough for a man of average height to stand up and move around in.

ous men, who attempted to pick out the worms, and after throwing out from fifty to eighty, stopped, not because the worms had come to an end, but because all the little bit of mush was going with them.

On Morris Island, we considered our selves in much more danger from the gun of the guard, than from our own Batteries.

The negroes were thick headed, and apt to misunderstand or go beyond their orders, they were therefore very dangerous.

Fortunately, they were miserable shots, else several men would have been killed, who really were not touched.

A Sutler was permitted to come in once a week, to sell Tobacco, Stationery, Molasses, Cakes, &c.—to those who had any money. Inside the enclosure and all around the tents, was a rope, this was the "Dead line[.]" To go beyond, or even to touch this rope, was death, that is if the Sentinel could hit you. When the Sutler came in, we were ordered to form in two ranks, faced by the flank toward the "Dead Line."

Every new comer had to fall in behind, and await his turn. On one occasion, a prisoner, either not knowing, or having forgotten the order, walked up to the "Dead line", on the flank of the line of men. An officer was standing by the Sentinel and ordered him to fire, which he did, and wonderful to say, missed not only the man at whom he shot, but the entire line. The officer then pulled out his pistol and fired. He also missed, and the prisoner, not relishing a position, where all the firing was on one side, made good his retreat to his tent.

Our authorities in Charleston, and the Yankee authorities on the Island, exchanged a boatload of provisions, Tobacco, &c for their respective prisoners. Bread, pot[at]oes, meat, and both chewing and smoking tobacco, were sent us by the Charleston ladies.

Never was any thing more enjoyed, and never I reckon, were men more thankful. I had enough to eat for once, even on Morris Island. The tobacco was a sweeter morsel, under the tongue and every man puffed out his wreaths of smoke with a keener relish, because "the Charleston ladies, God bless them, sent it."

Here as elsewhere, we were constantly expecting to be exchanged. No one laid any plan for longer than ten days, and at the end of that ten days—"Why we'll surely be in Dixie, before another ten days goes by."

One freak of the Yankees, I have never been able to account for. They took us out of the pen one morning, marched us down to the opposite end of the Island, put us on board two old hulks, kept us there for the night, and then marched us back to our old quarters.

About the 18th of October, we were ordered to be ready to leave early the next morning. In compliance with this order, we got up earlier than usual, to bundle up our few possessions and wash our faces before leaving. The Guard took this opportunity to shoot two of our number, one through the knee, the other in the shoulder.

Early in the morning of the 18th or 20th of Oct. we were drawn up in line. Three days rations were issued—viz fifteen "hard tack," and a right good sized piece of meat. I felt myself a rich man. I remember well the loving looks I cast upon my dear victuals and the tender care with which I adjusted and carried my trusty old haversack. A few moments more and we took up our line of march for the lower end of Morris Island, with a heavy line of dusky guard on either side. The distance was only three miles, but this to men confined for over a year, and for two months previous, subsisting upon such light rations, was a very considerable matter. Several of our number gave out completely, and had to be hauled the remaining distance.

Arrived at the wharf. Our negro guards were relieved by whites—The 157th N.Y. Vols Col. Brown[18] commanding. This officer and his men, though we were afterwards, while in their hands subjected to the most severe treatment, as far as they were individually concerned, treated us kindly.

We were put in two old "hulks" fitted up for us and then towed out to sea. The first evening of the journey, I fell upon my "victuals," and was so hungry, that I ate my three days rations at once. To a question from a friend, "What will you do for the rest of the time?" I replied, "I reckon the Lord will provide." But I made a mistake. I might have known the Almighty would use such instruments as were about us, only as ministers of wrath. The evening of the third day, we anchored off Fort Pulaski, situate[d] at the mouth of the Savannah river. By this time I was nearly famished. We did not land until the next morning, when we were marched into the Fort, & provisions given us. On the journey a party attempted to escape. They had succeeded in cutting a hole through the side of the vessel, and were just letting themselves down into the water when they were discovered. Fort Pulaski is a brick work, mounts two tiers of guns, the lower tier in casemates,[19] the walls enclose about an acre of ground. We were placed in the casemates, where bunks in the three tiers were

---

18. New York's 157th Infantry Regiment was led by Colonels Philip P. Brown and James C. Carmichael. It was organized in September 1862. See "157th Infantry Regiment, Civil War, Madison and Cortland Regiment," on *New York State Military Museum and Veterans Research Center* website, NYS Division of Military and Naval Affairs, November 17, 2009, https://dmna.ny.gov/historic/reghist/civil/infantry/157thInf/157thInfMain.htm.

19. Small rooms within the thickest parts of fortress walls where guns can also be fired.

prepared for us. The flooring was mostly brick, this was very damp, which together with the cold damp winds that prevailed during our stay rendered us very uncomfortable.

A heavy guard was thrown around our part of the Fort and for additional security, iron grates were placed in the embrasures.[20] Twenty prisoners at a time, were allowed to walk up and down the parade ground within the Fort for exercise. Doors & windows were generally kept shut, and our abiding place was dark and gloomy enough. Nothing remarkable happened until the end of the Old Year [1864]. A tolerable amount of rations was issued, and our life was pretty much the same with prison life elsewhere. The New Year brought a terrible change. General Foster (May he live for ever, where the Devil gets him) ordered us to be retaliated upon for alleged treatment of prisoners at Andersonville Ga. Our rations were reduced to less than a pint of meal, and about a half pint of pickle per day. No meat, and no vegetables of any kind were allowed us. The meal issued was damaged, it was in lumps larger than a man's head, it was sour, and generally filled with bugs and worms. We either had to eat this, or lie down and die at once. This regimen lasted 43 days. I cannot do justice to the misery and suffering experienced by myself, and seen everywhere around me, during this period. It is only one year since. And yet I can hardly believe I really passed through such scenes as memory brings before me.

Our diet soon induced Scurvy. This loathsome disease, in addition to the pangs of hunger, made life most insupportable. The disease first made its appearance in the mouth, loosening the teeth, and in many cases, making the gums a mass of black putrid flesh, it next attacked the limbs, appearing first in little spots, like blood blisters, one of which when broken, would become a hard, dark colored knot. These spots would increase until the whole limb was covered, by this time the muscles would contract and the limb be drawn beyond all power of straightening. I have seen not only the legs and arms but the *back* thus affected. Another feature of this disease, was the fainting produced by very slight exercise. I have walked down the prison, and stumbled upon men lying on the floor to all appearance dead, having fainted and fallen by exerting themselves to get to the "Sinks." Terrible as was the state of things, our sufferings were increased by as heartless and uncalled for a piece of cruelty as has ever been recorded.

---

20. Small openings in the wall of the casemates from which guns can be fired.

Our poor fellows generally were supplied and that scantily, with summer clothing, such as they brought from Fort Delaware in August. U.S. blankets (and many had no other kind)[21] had been taken away at Morris Island. Not only were *no* blankets nor clothing issued, but *we were not allowed to receive what friends had sent us.*

We had only so much fuel as was needed for cooking, starved almost to the point of death, a prey to disease, the blood in the veins so thin, that the least cold sent a shiver through the whole frame, no fire no blankets, scarcely any clothing. Can a more miserable existence be imagined? Add to this—the knowledge on our part that a few steps off—were those who lived in plenty and comfort. Crumbs and bones were there thrown daily to the dogs or carried to the dunghill, that would have made the eyes of the famished men in that prison glisten.

In consequence—the prisoners died like sheep. Whatever the immediate cause of their death—that cause was induced by starvation, and over the dead bones of nine tenths of those brave true men, can be given one verdict, *"Death by Starvation."*[22]

Suffering as I was myself, I remember an instance which touched me to the heart.

One poor fellow who grown too weak, to get off his bunk—said to his chum, "I can't stand this any longer, I must die." "O'no," said the other, "Cheer up man, rations will be issued again in two days, and I reckon they will certainly give us *something* to eat then. The poor fellow continued to live until the day for issuing rations, but it brought no change, the same short pint of damaged meal and pickles—and nothing more. As soon as the poor fellow heard this, he told his friend, not to beg him any more, for he could not live any longer. And the next evening—he died.

Fortunately for some of us—there were a great many cats about the prison and as may be imagined we were glad enough to eat cat. I have been partner in the killing and eating of three, and besides these, friends have frequently given me a share of their cat. We cooked them two ways—One we fried in his own fat for breakfast, another we baked

---

21. Either these blankets were issued to prisoners at one of the other prisons or Wash had been sleeping in a Union army blanket before his capture. The former explanation seems more likely, as Union prisoners often lost their blankets, among other things, to Confederates at the point of capture.

22. Nelson exaggerates the numbers here. According to the National Park Service, there are thirteen prisoner graves at Fort Pulaski. "SEAC: The Fort Pulaski Cemetery," on the National Park Service website, https://www.nps.gov/history/seac/research/fp/fp00010/2-civil_war/index-2.htm, accessed August 31, 2017.

with a stuffing & gravy, made of sour corn meal. My last was a kitten, tender and nice. A compassionate Yankee soldier gave it to me. I was cooking at the stove by the grating which separated us from the Guard. This soldier hailed me, 'I say—are you one of them fellers that eats cats!' I replied—"Yes[.]" ["]Well here is one I'll shove through if you want it." "Shove it through" I answered and in a very few minutes the kitten was in frying order.

Our guard were not allowed to relieve our sufferings, though they frequently expressed their sympathy. The Colonel himself told us it was a painful duty to inflict such suffering—but that we knew he was a soldier and must obey orders.

The 3rd of March 1865 dawned upon us ladened [*sic*] with rumors of a speedy exchange. The wings of hope had been so often clipped, one would have thought it impossible for her to rise very high. Yet each man was more or less excited. Strong protestations were heard on all sides—of belief that nothing would come of it, but the anxiety manifested in turning the rumor over and over, the criticisms upon the source from whence it came and the tenacity with which all clung to it in spite of processed disbelief showed that the hope of deliverance had sprung up in every heart. On the 4th the order came, to be ready to start in two hours. Soon after, one of our ranking officers was told by one of the Officials, that an order was just received from G^{enl} Grant[23] to exchange us immediately. We were wild with hope. The chilling despair which had settled upon us for some months—seemed to rise at once. All were busy packing their few articles. Cheerful talk and hearty laughter was heard all through the prison.

"Well, old fellow, off for Dixie at last," was said as often as one friend met another.

The alacrity with which the sick and crippled dragged themselves about, was wonderful.

Soon the drum beat. The line was formed, and the roll called, "Forward march" two by two we passed through the entrance of the Fort—over the moat—and then Fort Pulaski was left behind us for ever!

One sorrowful thought accompanied us. Our joy could not reach the poor fellows who had suffered with us and fallen victims to hunger and disease, and whose remains lay unhonored uncared for, aye unmarked. A good many head boards, with the name, rank and regiment of the dead had been prepared by friends, but an opportunity to put them up

---

23. General Ulysses S. Grant

Prisoners like Wash traveled by foot, rail, and water. Edwin
Forbes, *Rebel officers take[n] a[t] Petersburg, Va.—sketched on board
a steamboat coming down the James River, June 30, 1864*, Library of
Congress, http://www.loc.gov/pictures/item/2004661876/.

was not given, although it had been promised. We reached Hilton Head
without any[thing] of note happening. There we took on the rest of our
party—which had been sent here, at the beginning of the retaliation on
"Meal and Pickles" as we used to call it. This party had suffered the same
treatment. The greeting between friends was—"How are you, old fellow,
Ain't dead yet? You are hard to kill. I'm mighty glad to see you. Have
some pickles or here's sour meal—if you prefer it!" The boat in which we
started was now so crowded that there was not room for all to sit down.
It was so overloaded and "rolled" so, that the Captain refused to put to
sea, unless a larger ship were given him. Accordingly we were transferred
to the Steamship "Illinois". The sick, about half our number, occupied
the lower deck—the rest of us were packed away in the "Hold." But no
combination of circumstances could depress us so long as we believed
we were "bound for Dixie[.]" So we laughed at our close quarters, we
laughed at ourselves and at each other when sea sick. We were almost run
away with lice, but we [took] off shirts and skirmished with the varmints,
with the vim inspired by "Bound for Dixie."

We reached Fortress Monroe on the third day, I think. By this time, the filth in the ship was awful. Language can't describe the condition of the deck where the sick lay.

The poor fellows were unable to help themselves—and sea sickness and diarrhea had made their quarters unendurable. The stench was terrible. The air suffocating.

We expected to go right up the James river and be exchanged at City Point. But we were most cruelly disappointed. Orders were received to carry us to Fort Delaware. When we learned this, we were in despair. The stimulus which had enabled us to bear up all along was gone; we were utterly crushed. The dead of three of our number, during the day and night following, told the tale of our utter wretchedness. Their death excited little or no pity, I think the feeling excited, was rather one of envy. Those men in their hearts gave the lie to "the wearied and most wretched life, that age, ache, penury and imprisonment can lay on nature, is a paradise to what we fear in death."[24]

I remember hardly any thing about our passage from Fortress Monroe to Fort Delaware. A gloom too deep for even the ghost of hope to enter, was upon my spirits. I noticed little and cared less. Upon reaching Fort Delaware, seventy five of our number were carried to the prison hospital, and many more would have gone, had there been room. We were marched into the same place we had left more than six months before. I had no idea what a miserable looking set of men, we were, until I contrasted with the Fort Delaware prisoners, our old companions. I thought they were the fattest, best dressed set of men, I had ever seen.

That they looked thus to me, will excite no surprise—when I describe my own appearance. A flannel shirt, low in the neck, was my only under garment. An old overcoat, once white, was doing duty, as shirt, coat, and vest part of an old handkerchief tied round my head served as a hat. Breeches, I had none. An antiquated pair of red flannel drawers, endeavored, but with small success to supply their place. I was very thin and poor and was lame, scurvy having drawn the muscles of my right leg. When I add that I was in better condition, both in flesh and dress than many of our crowd, some idea can be formed—of the appearance we made.

---

24. Here Nelson must be quoting Shakespeare from memory, for he gets some of the quotation wrong. The passage, which is from *Measure for Measure* (act 3, scene 1), reads, "The weariest and most loathed worldly life / That age, ache, penury, and imprisonment / Can lay on nature, is a paradise / To what we fear of death."

The prisoners came to our rescue, gave us clothes, subscribed money and brought vegetables for us. For a long time after our arrival, when ever any one, was about to throw away an old crust of piece of meat or worn out garment, some bystander, would call out, "Don't throw that away, Give it to one of the poor Pulaski boys."

The fall of Richmond, Lee's surrender, and finally the capitulation of Johnston's army, soon swept from us every hope of a Southern Confederacy. But one course remained—viz to swear allegiance to the Government in whose power we were. Upon doing this, I was released on the 13th of June 1865.

Finis.

I wanted Wash to rewrite this, condensing a little and adding other items of great interest—but he says he can't. Some of the most touching incidents of his prison life were in connection with his letters—to which—naturally he does not choose to refer.

Mama had a letter in his handwriting—two days ago, beginning "Dear Grandmother" and announcing a little daughter. We wrote late at night, in fine spirits, after cutting wheat for a week, and the same prospect before him betimes next morning. I only got his final order to send this as it is to you then, and had to copy it in two "sittings" to be ready for to days mail. Please excuse errors as my hand is very tired.

Fannie M is here, and sends love, Charlie & Lanty set off yesterday for the ride through the valley. Lawny is comfortable and happy—she writes from the "Mountain top"

    Love to Pierrepont.

    Yours sincerely & aff—

    Jenny N.

July 14 1866
    Mt. Air

Acknowledgments

Like the letters between Wash and Mollie contained in this volume, this book came together as a collaborative process involving people separated by great distance. The project would not have been possible without the generous support from a number of colleagues across many institutions. We first must acknowledge Judkin Browning, whose interest in, and support of, publishing Wash and Mollie's writings has been invaluable from the beginning. Judkin read every word of the text and provided incisive comments that greatly improved our reading of the letters and memoir. He was also a model editor, giving his time for the improvement of the work throughout the entire editorial process.

The Center for Civil War Studies at Virginia Tech funded the initial research into the Nelson Family Papers. We thank Paul Quigley, in particular, for his enthusiastic support. The staff at Virginia Tech's Special Collections Library were instrumental in providing access to the original manuscripts as well as sharing the high-quality digital images of each item included in this volume. We thank Marc Brodsky, Aaron Purcell, and Kiera A. Dietz in particular for their assistance.

The Virginia Historical Society funded a separate research trip that resulted in locating Wash's 1866 memoir. At the Virginia Historical Society, we benefited from assistance from the reference staff, especially John McClure, as well as E. Lee Shepard, vice president for collections, who gave us permission to include the memoir in the volume.

Several colleagues gave assistance throughout the process of editing this volume. In particular, we are grateful to Peter S. Carmichael for research tips and recommendations. He introduced us to Robert Krick, historian at the Richmond National Battlefield Park, for example, whose insight into Hanover County, Virginia, was especially helpful to us. We are also grateful for support from two experts on Civil War prisons: Glenn Robins, who read and commented on parts of the manuscript, and Roger Pickenpaugh, who read the entire manuscript. Their expertise and diligent copyediting significantly improved our work. The staff at Andersonville National Historic Site, especially park ranger Jennifer Hopkins, provided quick reference and useful feedback along the way.

Likewise, John and Teresa Walther, two traveling "Volunteers in Parks," read an early version of the manuscript while one of us (Evan) worked as a seasonal park ranger at Andersonville. Wade Barr generously reviewed our genealogical work. We are grateful not only for the invaluable research assistance but also for all those whose profession is interpreting the tougher parts of American history and memory.

Students at the Robert D. Clark Honors College (University of Oregon) read early drafts of the letters in class and offered invaluable insight as well as provocative questions that shaped how we ultimately framed the sources. We must also thank Bryan Crosby, a history student at Georgia Southwestern State University, for early work on this book's companion website as part of a public history class project.

Finally, we must thank the staff of the University of Georgia Press, especially Mick Gusinde-Duffy and Jon Davies, our thorough copyeditor, Aden Nichols, and the two anonymous readers of the manuscript. We are thrilled to make a small contribution to this new series.

Select Bibliography

Anderson, John Nathan. "Money or Nothing: Confederate Postal System Collapse during the Civil War." *American Journalism* 30, no. 1 (Winter 2013): 65–86.

Atchison, Ray M. "'The Land We Love': A Southern Post-Bellum Magazine of Agriculture, Literature, and Military History." *North Carolina Historical Review* 37, no. 4 (1960): 506–15.

Ayers, Edward L., Gary W. Gallagher, and Andrew J. Torget, eds. *Crucible of the Civil War: Virginia from Secession to Commemoration.* Charlottesville, Va.: University of Virginia Press, 2006.

Barber, Susan. "'The White Wings of Eros': Courtship and Marriage in Confederate Richmond." In *Southern Families at War: Loyalty and Conflict in the Civil War South,* edited by Catherine Clinton. Oxford, England: Oxford University Press, 2000.

Berry, Stephen William. *All That Makes a Man: Love and Ambition in the Civil War South.* New York: Oxford University Press, 2003.

———. "When Mail Was Armor: Envelopes of the Great Rebellion, 1861–1865." *Southern Cultures* 4, no. 3 (1998): 63.

Blight, David W. *Race and Reunion: The Civil War in American Memory.* Cambridge, Mass: Belknap Press of Harvard University Press, 2002.

Boyd, Steven R. *Patriotic Envelopes of the Civil War: The Iconography of Union and Confederate Covers.* Baton Rouge: Louisiana State University Press, 2010.

Brockway, A. N., ed. *Catalogue of the Delta Kappa Epsilon Fraternity.* New York: Council Publishing Company, 1900.

Bush, David R., ed. *I Fear I Shall Never Leave This Island: Life in a Civil War Prison.* Gainesville: University of Florida Press, 2011.

Bushong, Millard Kessler. *A History of Jefferson County, West Virginia.* Bowie, Md.: Heritage Books, 2002.

Carmichael, Peter S. *The Last Generation: Young Virginians in Peace, War, And Reunion.* Chapel Hill: University of North Carolina Press, 2005.

Cartmell, T. K. *Shenandoah Valley Pioneers and Their Descendants: A History of Frederick County, Virginia from Its Formation in 1738 to 1908.* Winchester, Va.: Eddy Press Corp., 1909.

Cloyd, Benjamin G. *Haunted by Atrocity: Civil War Prisons in American Memory.* Baton Rouge: Louisiana State University Press, 2010.

Cocke, William Ronald. *Hanover County Chancery Wills and Notes: A Compendium of Genealogical, Biographical and Historical Material as Contained in Cases of the*

Chancery Suits of Hanover County, Virginia. Columbia, Va.: William Ronald Cocke III, 1940.

Dabney, Virginius. *Richmond: The Story of a City.* Charlottesville, Va.: University of Virginia Press, 1990. First published 1976 by Doubleday.

Faust, Drew Gilpin. *Mothers of Invention: Women of the Slaveholding South in the American Civil War.* Chapel Hill: University of North Carolina Press, 1996.

Foster, Gaines M. *Ghosts of the Confederacy: Defeat, the Lost Cause, and the Emergence of the New South, 1865 to 1913.* New York: Oxford University Press, 1987.

Glatthaar, Joseph. *Soldiering in the Army of Northern Virginia: A Statistical Portrait of the Troops Who Served under Robert E. Lee.* Chapel Hill: University of North Carolina Press, 2011.

Harris, M. Keith. *Across the Bloody Chasm: The Culture of Commemoration among Civil War Veterans.* Baton Rouge: Louisiana State University Press, 2014.

Harris, William Samuel. *The Harris Family, Thomas Harris, in Ipswich, Mass. In 1636. And Some of His Descendants, through Seven Generations, to 1883.* Nashua, N.H.: Barker & Bean, 1883.

Hesseltine, William Best. *Civil War Prisons: A Study in War Psychology.* Columbus: Ohio State University Press, 1930; rpt. Columbus: Ohio State University Press, 1998.

Jabour, Anya. *Scarlett's Sisters: Young Women in the Old South.* Chapel Hill: University of North Carolina Press, 2007.

Kelley, Mary. *Learning to Stand & Speak: Women, Education, and Public Life in America's Republic.* Chapel Hill: Published for the Omohundro Institute of Early American History and Culture, Williamsburg, Virginia, by the University of North Carolina Press, 2006.

Link, William A. *Roots of Secession: Slavery and Politics in Antebellum Virginia.* Chapel Hill: University of North Carolina Press, 2003.

Lystra, Karen. *Searching the Heart: Women, Men, and Romantic Love in Nineteenth-Century America.* New York: Oxford University Press, 1989.

Moore II. Robert H. *Miscellaneous Disbanded Virginia Light Artillery.* Lynchburg, Va.: H. E. Howard, Inc., 1997.

Morrison, A. J. *The Beginnings of Public Education in Virginia, 1776–1860; Study of Secondary Schools in Relation to the State Literary Fund.* Richmond: Davis Pottom, Superintendent of Public Printing, 1917.

Nelson, Megan Kate. *Ruin Nation: Destruction and the American Civil War.* UnCivil Wars. Athens: University of Georgia Press, 2012.

Ott, Victoria E. *Confederate Daughters: Coming of Age during the Civil War.* Carbondale: Southern Illinois University Press, 2008.

Page, Richard Channing Moore. *Genealogy of the Page Family in Virginia. Also a Condensed Account of the Nelson, Walker, Pendelton and Randolph Families.* 1893.

Phillips, Jason. *Diehard Rebels: The Confederate Culture of Invincibility.* Athens: University of Georgia Press, 2007.

———. "The Grape Vine Telegraph: Rumors and Confederate Persistence." *The Journal of Southern History* 72, no. 4 (November 1, 2006): 753–88.

Pickenpaugh, Roger. *Captives in Gray: The Civil War Prisons of the Union.* Tuscaloosa: University of Alabama Press, 2009.

———. *Johnson's Island: A Prison for Confederate Officers.* Kent, Ohio: Kent State University Press, 2016.

Rubin, Anne S. *A Shattered Nation: The Rise and Fall of the Confederacy, 1861–1868.* Civil War America. Chapel Hill: University of North Carolina Press, 2005.

Runge, William H., ed. *Four Years in the Confederate Artillery: The Diary of Private Henry Robinson Berkeley.* Chapel Hill: Published for the Virginia Historical Society by the University of North Carolina Press, 1961.

Sodergren, Steven E. "'The Great Weight of Responsibility': The Struggle over History and Memory in Confederate Veteran Magazine." *Southern Cultures* 19, no. 3 (2013): 26–45.

Starnes, Richard D. "Forever Faithful: The Southern Historical Society and Confederate Historical Memory." *Southern Cultures* 2, no. 2 (1996): 177–94.

Sternhell, Yael A. "Communicating War: The Culture of Information in Richmond during the American Civil War." *Past and Present* 202, no. 1 (2009): 175–205.

Taylor, James E. *With Sheridan up the Shenandoah Valley in 1864: Leaves from a Special Artist's Sketchbook and Diary.* Cleveland, Ohio: Western Reserve Historical Society, 1989.

"The Treatment of Prisoners During the War between the States." *Southern Historical Society Papers,* 1, no. 3 (March, 1876): 113–327.

Turner, Charles W., ed. *The Prisoner of War Letters of Lieutenant Thomas Dix Houston (1863–65).* Verona, Va.: McClure Printing Company, 1980.

Varon, Elizabeth R. *We Mean to Be Counted: White Women & Politics in Antebellum Virginia.* Chapel Hill: University of North Carolina Press, 1998.

Waugh, Charles G. and Martin H. Greenberg, eds., *The Women's War in the South: Recollections and Reflections of the American Civil War.* Nashville, Tenn.: Cumberland House, 1999.

Whites, LeeAnn. "The Civil War as a Crisis in Gender." In *Divided Houses: Gender and the Civil War,* edited by Catherine Clinton and Nina Silber, 3–21. New York: Oxford University Press, 1992.

Williams, Timothy J. *Intellectual Manhood: University, Self, and Society in the Antebellum South.* Chapel Hill: University of North Carolina Press, 2015.

Wonders, Katarina. "Prisoner of War: George Washington Nelson." Unpublished manuscript, on the Long Branch Plantation official website, accessed April 23, 2017, http://www.visitlongbranch.org/history/archives/

Wyatt-Brown, Bertram. *The Shaping of Southern Culture: Honor, Grace, and War, 1760s–1890s.* Chapel Hill: University of North Carolina Press, 2001.

———. *Southern Honor: Ethics and Behavior in the Old South.* New York: Oxford University Press, 1982.

Index

New Perspectives on the Civil War

Printed in the United States
By Bookmasters